Building CLASSROOM READING Communities

This book is dedicated to the amazing readers in the "little classroom." Thank you for teaching us that RMA and Socratic Circles are a perfect fit for young children learning about themselves as readers and as members of a community of readers.

Building CLASSROOM READING Communities

Retrospective Miscue Analysis and Socratic Circles

RITA A. MOORE • VICTORIA N. SEEGER

Foreword by Dorothy Watson

CORWIN
A SAGE Company

Note: Most of the students' names within this book are pseudonyms; however, there are two exceptions. The students' names were preserved on work artifacts reproduced in their original form within the text. In Chapter 13, we have included discussions with two students Vicki worked with one year later. Their actual names appear in the text.

For information:

Corwin
A SAGE Company
2455 Teller Road
Thousand Oaks, California 91320
(800) 233-9936
Fax: (800) 417-2466
www.corwinpress.com

SAGE India Pvt. Ltd.
B 1/I 1 Mohan Cooperative
Industrial Area
Mathura Road, New Delhi 110 044
India

SAGE Ltd.
1 Oliver's Yard
55 City Road
London EC1Y 1SP
United Kingdom

SAGE Asia-Pacific Pte. Ltd.
33 Pekin Street #02-01
Far East Square
Singapore 048763

Printed in the United States of America

Library of Congress Cataloging-in-Publication Data

Moore, Rita A.
Building classroom reading communities: retrospective miscue analysis and socratic circles/ Rita A. Moore, Victoria N. Seeger; foreword by Dorothy Watson.
p. cm.
Includes bibliographical references and index.
ISBN 978-1-4129-6800-3 (cloth)
ISBN 978-1-4129-6801-0 (pbk.)
1. Miscue analysis. 2. Reading. 3. Group reading. 4. Questioning. 5. Critical thinking. I. Title.

LB1050.33.M65 2010
372.41'62—dc22 2009035715

This book is printed on acid-free paper.

09 10 11 12 13 10 9 8 7 6 5 4 3 2 1

Acquisitions Editor: Cathy Hernandez
Editorial Assistant: Sarah Bartlett
Production Editor: Eric Garner
Copy Editor: Jeannette McCoy
Typesetter: C&M Digitals (P) Ltd.
Proofreader: Carole Quandt
Indexer: Sheila Bodell
Cover Designer: Scott Van Atta
Graphic Designer: Karine Hovsepian

Contents

List of Figures

Foreword

Building Classroom Reading Communities: Retrospective Miscue Analysis (RMA) and Socratic Circles

Dorothy Watson

> *. . . we sought to involve the entire class in RMA discussions. (It is important to suggest "full" class, as this is one of the most vital points to our version of RMA.)*

To put it mildly, those words captured my attention.

The search for a classroom community in which mixed-ability students are fully engaged in becoming better readers is a quest Rita Moore and Vicki Seeger pursued and now share in these pages. Through the use of Retrospective Miscue Analysis (RMA) within a classroom community of Socratic Circles (SC), the authors lead us in the investigation of an exciting literacy experience for readers. They help us consider ways of inviting students to explore their language, ways of motivating readers to pose and ponder questions, and even ways of including parents in the experience.

RMA grew out of Kenneth Goodman's research into students' reading and his consequent theory that reading is a meaning-making literacy event. RMA is grounded in Goodman's work and developed by Yetta Goodman as an *evaluation tool* in which readers participate in the examination of their attempts to make meaning from a variety of texts. RMA is also an *inquiry strategy* that engages readers in the investigation of their strengths and needs. Within the social context of SCs, thought-provoking conversations emerge about text and involve students in helping themselves and their peers become more insightful readers by way of supportive questioning and discussions about their reading. SCs help students become aware that there is more than one way of tackling a problem and to understand that sometimes answering a question by asking a related question helps them think for themselves rather than waiting for the teacher to tell them what and how to think.

By bringing together the two powerful strategies of RMA and SCs, the authors unite a means and a setting by which creative thinking and critical reflection can emerge. Through RMA, students pay attention to and value their own past and current life experiences, especially their reading experiences, and they relate their prior knowledge with new knowledge they are gaining. Within the safe and inviting SCs, there are no longer invisible students, *all* readers are free to question themselves and their peers, to search for connections to other texts, connections across the curriculum, and to do something they may never have considered doing in the past—to question authors' writing styles, vocabulary, and points of view.

Through reflection and discussion of their reading abilities and problems, students become more serious and sensitive readers. With the help of each other and their teacher, they realize that as they investigate their reading, *strategies for making sense of what and how they are reading* become increasingly evident and usable. In addition to becoming aware of their growing power as readers, students also realize why and how their ability is increasing, and they are eager to share their newly gained knowledge and successes with others. The ability to articulate what they are doing gives students a firmer handle on the reading process. Similarly, RMA within SCs helps teachers clarify and articulate their curricular strategies, consequently strengthening themselves as teachers and researchers of the reading process and literacy curriculum.

The authors present powerful and telling vignettes in which we see students seeking the opinions of their classmates, and as a result, unraveling puzzling reading issues. Within SCs children seek and offer insightful advice based on their own struggles and successes with reading. We see students developing sharper listening skills, consequently increasing their respect for the abilities and needs of others. The vignettes show a growing democratic community in which students are eager to participate and are at all times respectful of others.

We know, through Ken Goodman's research followed by the research of myriads of educators, that with the understanding of miscue analysis comes the realization that we will never view reading in the same way again. Our authors propose that when we experience the combined power of RMA and SCs, we may never teach in the same way again.

Rita and Vicki have ventured into a challenging and creative learning experience in which important cognitive and social abilities are fostered and celebrated. Through the pages of their book, they invite all educators (preservice, special education, and classroom teachers; administrators, teacher educators, researchers, and parents) to join them in a stimulating and thought-provoking experience.

Preface

RMA: An Effective Design for Elementary Literacy Curriculum

> *Miscue analysis is a powerful tool that gives teachers and students a "window on the reading process."*
>
> —Ken Goodman, *Miscue Analysis: Applications to Reading Instruction*

BACKGROUND

Since the early 1960s miscue analysis has been studied and used in the evaluation and teaching of reading. Retrospective Miscue Analysis (RMA) is an extension of miscue analysis that involves readers in discussing their oral reading and retelling miscues with teachers and/or other classmates. This book is largely based on the use of RMA in Vicki Seeger's third-grade classroom; however, it touches on the research and work of others as well.

Vicki and Rita both have a history with RMA. Vicki, once a graduate student in some of Rita's classes at the university, is also a literacy coach and former classroom teacher. She has consistently used RMA as a procedure for teaching reading for over five years. Rita, a university professor and former K–12 reading specialist, has studied the use of RMA with struggling readers for over 10 years. We have eagerly joined the growing number of teachers who are trying RMA with success and enthusiasm in teaching reading. We believe that successful readers understand the reading process and the strategies that support it. Having the chance to articulate the process of reading with others helps struggling readers become more effective readers. We have learned that the discussion of reading miscues during RMA opens the door for informed, interesting discussions about reading that explores vocabulary development, comprehension, critical thinking, and fluency, also recognized as integral components of critical literacy.

THE RMA PROCESS

Retrospective Miscue Analysis (RMA) is a simple process of organizing readers for conversations about reading miscues and retellings. It has two parts: the analysis of miscues and the examination of the retelling of text. The rest of this work explains in much greater detail the process and outcomes of RMA. The following brief introduction to RMA provides a refresher for those familiar with RMA and lays a foundation for those who are not. While we assume that readers will begin with Chapter 1 and read straight through, those who are more experienced in miscue analysis and RMA may be most interested in how Vicki harnessed the power of RMA for full class literacy instruction.

As most teachers will know, miscues are unexpected responses to text. For RMA, miscues are carefully collected and organized by the teacher to guide discussion during small reading groups. Figure 0.1 provides a quick overview of how to prepare for and conduct RMA.

Figure 0.1 Steps to Implement RMA in the Classroom

Steps to Prepare for Implementation of RMA

Step 1: Identify students for RMA groups based on reading skills and needs.

Step 2: Explain the words "Retrospective Miscue Analysis" and tell what it is and how a session is conducted. Why miscues are made and what they are should be part of the explanation. However, this should be brief because it can be expanded upon later while students are actually in the process.

Step 3: Display an RMA poster (chart paper) in the classroom that identifies the common miscues, smart and okay miscues, and a reminder to make connections while discussing.

Step 4: Set up an RMA recording literacy station in the classroom.

Step 5: Make RMA folders for each reader. Folders include a cassette tape and a copy of the text the student will be reading into the tape recorder.

Step 6: Model an RMA discussion using one or two students in the classroom with their prior permission.

Steps to Conduct RMA in the Classroom

Step 1: Select text for each group of readers. Enlarge the text or retype it. Use line identification numbers in the margins.

Step 2:	Explain tape-recording process so that students can record themselves reading text.
Step 3:	Transcribe recordings.
Step 4:	Copy transcribed miscues for each member of each RMA group.
Step 5:	Conduct RMA discussion sessions.

Prior to the group discussion, the teacher listens to previously recorded readings of the text by group members and analyzes the miscues of each reader. (The recording is conducted in literacy stations prior to the discussion.) These teacher-selected miscues are provided on paper to members of the small group who are encouraged and empowered to discuss the meaning behind the miscues in thoughtful, respectful ways with one another. The second part of RMA is the retelling. This is a comprehension check strategy during which the reader literally "re-tells" what is remembered about the text. The group listens to the recorded retelling of each of the group members, then they are invited to discuss what they heard after each retelling as the teacher facilitates the discussion. Subsequent chapters will demonstrate how to prepare a classroom and students for RMA.

AN EFFECTIVE APPROACH TO CRITICAL LITERACY

Both miscues and retellings are viewed as "windows into the reading process" (Goodman, 1973) by the teacher and students rather than as comprehension errors to be constantly corrected. Examining how the brain works during reading provides the genesis for RMA and leads to clarifying conversations about vocabulary and word choice, spelling, the author's style, punctuation, background knowledge linked to the miscue or retelling, comprehension, and fluency. In short, it is exciting, scientific, and most of all, as empowering for readers who learn that miscues have meaning as it is for teachers who use what is learned during RMA to make sound, data-informed instructional choices.

RMA THE SOCRATIC WAY

We learned from previous work that all readers can benefit from RMA discussions so we wondered how we could effectively share the outcomes of individual RMA groups with the entire class. After some initial practice, we modified the method of Socratic Circles (SC) used in high school classrooms (Copeland, 2005) to provide an organizational framework and discussion technique for elementary children. Essentially, large groups "listened in" on small group RMA discussions, and later group members constructively commented on what they had heard that gave them a deeper understanding of "what readers do" when they read. We were amazed at how seriously the third graders, a mixed group of abilities and backgrounds, carried out their responsibilities during RMA and how excited they were to have ownership in the teaching and learning process. This excitement motivated the development of classroom reading communities.

We are grateful to the children who participated in RMA throughout our work as reading teachers and have included classroom RMA conversations from the third graders to highlight the main ideas covered in each chapter of the book. We believe these conversations clearly express the thinking of the children as they learned to "speak RMA." We invite teachers trying RMA for the first time to share the vignettes of the third graders with other young readers as they prepare them for RMA conversations.

Throughout the book, we cite the research grounding our work and include a complete review of the research in a separate section: Resource A. We feel privileged to write this book about our experiences with the third-grade readers and to share our beliefs and passion about the power of language in teaching reading. It is our hope that readers will take away some ideas for introducing RMA into their literacy curricula.

The chapters that follow are intended for teachers, future teachers, parents, or administrators who are interested in authentic, meaningful literacy education that really "works." Chapter 1 introduces and defines RMA; Chapter 2 grounds the RMA process firmly in literacy theory and practice; Chapter 3 explains how the reading process may be connected to miscue analysis; Chapter 4 demonstrates the marking and coding of miscues; Chapter 5 explains how to organize the classroom for RMA; Chapter 6 explores the use of RMA for assessing reading; Chapter 7 suggests ways of informing instruction through RMA; Chapter 8 explains how the use of RMA groups may be integrated into all aspects of the classroom literacy program; Chapter 9 explains how Socratic Circles may assist in involving the entire classroom community in RMA conversations and learning; Chapters 10, 11, and 12 provide examples of how RMA "works" with striving, developing and proficient readers; and Chapter 13 presents some concluding thoughts and two follow-up interviews with two students in Vicki's third-grade classroom. Resource A provides a summary of the research relative to miscue analysis and RMA.

We invite teachers, aspiring teachers, parents, and administrators to consider the use of RMA in their literacy curriculum, and as we did with the use of Socratic Circles, find new ways of managing RMA groups as communities of learners and readers. It is our hope that you enjoy the book and take from it ideas that you may use in your school or with your own children. There are no mandates and no prescribed texts—just good teaching ideas grounded in years of research.

—Rita Moore and Vicki Seeger

Acknowledgments

Corwin gratefully acknowledges the contributions of the following reviewers:

Diane Brantley, Associate Professor of Literacy Education
Department of Language, Literacy, and Culture
California State University, San Bernardino
San Bernardino, CA

Charla Bunker, Fifth-Grade Teacher
West Elementary School
Sun River, MT

Tracy Carbone, Literacy Facilitator
Villa Heights Elementary School
Indian Trail, NC

Rebecca Compton, Professor of Elementary Education
East Central University
Ada, OK

Catherine Compton-Lilly, Professor of Literacy
University of Wisconsin
Madison, WI

Carol Gallegos, Literacy Coach
Hanford Elementary School District
Lemoore, CA

Louanne Jacobs, Assistant Professor of Reading and Literacy
Alabama A&M University
Madison, AL

Sharon Jefferies, Third-Grade Teacher
Lakeville Elementary School
Orlando, FL

Stephanie Malin, Literacy Coach
Nancy Ryles Elementary School
Beaverton, OR

Natalie S. McAvoy, Reading Specialist
Tibbets Elementary School
Elkhorn, WI

Kay Teehan, Literacy Coach
Bartow Middle School
Lakeland, FL

Betty Yundt, Fifth-Grade Teacher
Walker Intermediate School
Fort Knox, KY

About the Authors

Rita A. Moore

Victoria N. Seeger

Rita A. Moore, PhD and **Victoria N. Seeger**, MA are former classroom teachers. Vicki, a veteran public school teacher of 14 years, is now a literacy coach for a large school district in Topeka, Kansas, as well as an adjunct instructor at Washburn University in Topeka. Rita, a former Title I reading teacher and high school language arts teacher is a Professor of Education and Associate Dean at Willamette University in Salem, Oregon. Both have worked continuously together since 2001 on research, including professional development schools, classroom research for teachers, and RMA from which they have coauthored several articles. In addition, Vicki contributed to the book *Reading Conversations: RMA With Struggling Readers Grades 4–12* (2004) coauthored by Rita Moore and Carol Gilles. Vicki regularly conducts professional development workshops on literacy strategies and curriculum development in the Seaman 345 School District in Topeka. She has also served as consultant to preservice literacy education classrooms through the University of Montana-Western. In addition to *Reading Conversations* (2005), Rita has written *Classroom Research for*

Teachers: A Practical Guide (2004) and has published over 30 articles in peer-reviewed journals on topics related to literacy education and the preparation of preservice teachers.

Rita Moore holds a master's degree in reading from Southwest Missouri University, and a PhD in literacy education from the University of Missouri-Columbia. Vicki holds a masters degree in education from Washburn University and finishes her PhD in literacy curriculum and instruction from Kansas State University in Manhattan, Kansas, in the fall of 2009. Both are dedicated to the notion that the integral and often seamless connectivity between language and literacy defines us as human beings and empowers us as learners.

1

Revaluing Readers

Introducing RMA

I told you. I can't read . . . just check my test scores! You'll see.

—Watson, 2008

This chapter will do the following:

- Provide an introduction to the rest of the book
- Present the traditional and current trends in Retrospective Miscue Analysis (RMA)
- Highlight the value of miscue analysis and RMA to teachers and readers

INTRODUCTION

In a recent National Council for Teachers of English (NCTE) summer institute, Dorothy Watson presented some of her most recent work with young readers who did not conceive of themselves as successful readers. One youngster, after Dorothy patiently tried to get him to tell her what kind of reader he thought he was, finally said not without some aggravation, "I told you. I can't read . . . just check my test scores! You'll see" (Watson, 2008). In listening to Watson's stories about children who clearly knew what it was to be a good reader but did not characterize themselves as such, we are reminded that the reason for exploring language and miscues with children is to empower the reader to understand that reading is a process not a subject to be taught. Everyone may learn to read differently, and every reader's interpretation of text is grounded in his or her personal and social identities. Finding ways of showing readers that reading is making sense of text, not getting one phoneme at a time, is at the heart of RMA discussions.

The idea for inviting whole-class participation in small-group reading conversations about their oral reading miscues and retellings evolved from an experience that Vicki had with her fifth-grade class the previous year. Struggling readers were grouped to discuss their miscues and retellings; Vicki facilitated these groups while the rest of the students were supposed to be working on other assignments. Instead, she found those not involved in the RMA reading groups more interested in what was being said in the reading groups than in other work. Vicki recalled how later her more proficient readers asked if they could also talk about their miscues and retellings and the meanings behind them. The results were so positive that we decided to develop a strategy that would allow Vicki to set up RMA conversations among all the readers in Vicki's new third-grade classroom. We organized it so that there were regular opportunities for all reading groups to listen to one another's discussions about miscues of pronunciation and meaning using the inner and outer circle models associated with the original Socratic Circle model (Copeland, 2005). The results were empowering and built classroom community like nothing we have seen before. How miscues are gathered and organized for RMA conversations and how these conversations are shared with the entire classroom community are explained and explored in subsequent chapters.

TRADITIONAL AND CURRENT TRENDS IN RMA

There have been many studies and uses of RMA in classrooms since the mid-1970s, but to our knowledge, RMA was never paired with Socratic Circle methods. Traditional RMA adheres to the principles held by Yetta Goodman and Ann Marek (1996). It was designed to be an evaluation tool for an adult student's oral reading and associated thinking processes, the purpose being to *revalue* what the reader knows about reading and strengths the student brings to the acts that take place during reading. In the tradition of miscue analysis, the term *evaluation* was redefined within the paradigm that values the reader. In addition, we define assessment as a "continuous examination" or a continuum of reflecting, assessing, and evaluation of each reader's progress much like the approach used by Kathleen and James Strickland (2000).

RMA has evolved from a protocol to be administered by a teacher with an adult struggling reader to an assessment and teaching strategy that may be used to support a range of reading abilities. RMA can be adapted to any classroom environment dependent on the needs of the students and the teacher's purpose for using RMA. In the past, Rita used RMA with struggling readers who puzzled their teachers. Her experiences were primarily through what are commonly called "pull out" programs where small classes of students are taught literacy skills in small groups.

Vicki too has used RMA in this manner as well as in private tutoring sessions; however, in a classroom, RMA can be used with a group of readers who struggle or with the entire class, as demonstrated in this book. Vicki implemented RMA with a small group of struggling readers in previous years. Each of the readers within the group brought unique strengths to the discussions because all of the readers struggled in different ways but were also successful in diverse ways. The insights those readers offered to their peers in RMA discussions were remarkable even though the students seemed an unlikely mix of abilities. In this book, we invite readers to consider the many ways that RMA may be integrated into literacy instruction in any traditional classroom setting. Its use is flexible.

The RMA process we are discussing in this book has roots in traditional RMA—particularly the underlying beliefs that the process values and empowers the reader. Differences are structural and include students being responsible for tape-recording their own readings of the text along with the retelling rather than with a teacher present. After reviewing the tapes and marking miscues for discussion, readers are provided with an organized protocol and the opportunity to discuss the miscues that the teacher has highlighted and others they notice. Vicki facilitates the discussion providing further probing and guidance only when needed. This process is sometimes referred to as CRMA or Collaborative Retrospective Miscue Analysis explained further in the work of Moore and Gilles (2005). The emphasis in CRMA is on students collaboratively discussing their miscues with the teacher moving from group to group to listen to discussions or take notes on what is said. It may also be compared to Over the Shoulder Miscue Reflection (Davenport & Lauritzen, 2002), which takes on similar aspects of teacher-reader participation and conversation. In traditional RMA, the teacher in collaboration with a single student discussed oral reading miscues as they listened to previously recorded readings of the reader. While the benefits are well established for traditional RMA, the process we describe in this book involves small group discussions among readers we characterize as "developing, striving, and proficient readers." Each student belongs to an RMA group, and RMA is part of the overall literacy curriculum.

The process we adopted is actually based on Dorothy Watson's (1978) early work in Reader-Selected Miscues (RSM). Watson, a pioneer in miscue and retrospective miscue, has worked with hundreds of children as they listened to their reading and discovered themselves as readers. We believe her work may predate some of the work of Goodman and Marek in that it first introduced the notion of readers selecting their own miscues for discussion as a means of valuing and empowering the reader's participation in the literacy and learning process.

In the process of RMA we use, the RSM are those that the readers choose to focus on during the discussion time based on what they have plausible explanations for or concerns about as they reflect on their reading. As in RSM, hearing from the readers about their miscues, their interpretations of text, and their understanding of what "works" for them as readers (Watson, personal communication, March 15, 1995) frames our presentation of RMA. In addition to the reader's voice, peers are invited to contribute to possible explanations of miscues from their own reading experiences and perspectives. Together, the discussions held within the group enrich the students' awareness of reading miscues and retellings. We have found this approach to literacy acquisition and reading in general demonstrates to students that reading is an ongoing, cognitive process that develops over time based on knowledge and experiences rather than a discrete set of skills to be mastered. Efficacy in reading rests on the extent of the reader's prior knowledge and experience with language. Talking about and sharing knowledge and experiences with language benefits all readers and makes it much easier for teachers to demonstrate the value of reading across the curriculum.

THE VALUE OF MISCUE ANALYSIS AND RMA TO TEACHERS AND READERS

Teachers who have conducted miscue analysis on children's oral reading and retellings never listen to children or adults read in the same way again. They hear reading miscues that provide insight into what the reader is thinking about as one reads. Here's a quick example: One young reader read "caffeine table" for "coffee table" then quickly corrected his miscue. When asked why he might have made that substitution he replied, "Because coffee has caffeine in it." RMA extends the invitation of linguistic exploration to all readers, empowering them to examine for themselves the reading process and how they utilize knowledge of language, culture, and experience to interact with the text as they read.

Those teachers who have not conducted miscue analysis need to know that miscues are a different way of looking at reading errors. Miscues are missed, misinterpreted, or misunderstood cues of language. They occur because a reader is struggling to make meaning from the text. In this way of thinking, they are "unexpected responses to text" that may or may not alter the meaning significantly. While there are subtle nuances of meaning associated with any reading substitution, when the miscue does not fundamentally change the meaning of the sentence, it is called a high-level or *smart* miscue. A *low-level* or *okay* miscue may change the meaning of the sentence but still maintains the readers' ability to move ahead because it acts as a placeholder. To varying degrees, low-level miscues change the meaning of the sentence, but proficient readers will likely correct low-level miscues as they continue to read. When encouraged to talk about these miscues, less proficient readers learn how to recognize and correct low-level miscues. Miscues are not mistakes; they are linguistic occurrences that always provide teachers with a glimpse into how the brain works to make sense of the written word.

As you will see in subsequent chapters, particularly Chapter 4, miscues of word recognition are discussed during RMA conversations as readers postulate reasons for the miscue, such as "the words *house* and *home* look similar, and some people say, 'Come over to my house' and mean 'Come over to my home.'" Rich discussions about tone, meaning, and various nuances of language such as code switching and dialect engage readers as they discuss and compare their individual miscues. The discussion then ranges to the retellings of text, noting interpretations, details, miscues of understanding, and so much more.

Valuing the Reader's Strengths

The RMA process guides instruction in a fluid, authentic manner. The reader is a full participant in the process. During a recent online discussion among reading professionals, Yetta Goodman (2007) explains the value of miscue analysis:

> Miscue analysis shows us how smart the brain is as it reads a whole story or article or headline. . . . Teachers discover that readers know grammar as they substitute the same part of speech that is in the written story or article. They discover that kids are predicting what is going to happen next in the sentence based on what they already know as learners. Or the prediction fits with the sentence up to the miscue and the reader stops, hesitates, and/or self-corrects. Teachers find out that readers are monitoring what they are reading—searching for meaning when they self-correct a prediction that was acceptable up to the point of miscue. . . . These show readers' strengths.

When teachers know readers' strengths, they begin to build on the strengths rather than focus on weaknesses. For example, a child strong in word recognition may not always have proficient recall of the text. Building on word recognition, talking about the word, and asking the reader if the word makes sense in a specific context helps the reader develop a sense of organization while reading. The work of Keene and Zimmerman (1997, 2007) strongly reflects the notion that proficient readers know how to use comprehension strategies like these. For some, developing effective reading strategies comes naturally, but for others, they must be learned and supported. RMA provides the structure for that support.

The reading process is all about strategies for making meaning. Think about what you do as you pick up a book you have long wanted to read or one that you may not be sure you want to buy. The strategies all readers rely upon, regardless of language or culture, when they begin to read a text are sampling, predicting, and confirming (or self-correcting if the prediction was wrong). The systems of language that will be explained further in Chapter 2, including the graphophonic system (graphics and sounds), the semantic system (meaning), and the syntactic system (grammar), support these strategies. The reader sticks with the word if it makes sense semantically and syntactically.

REFLECTION

Teachers who use RMA in their regular reading instruction see marked changes in their students' critical thinking processes as well as their understanding of reading. Students begin to realize that reading is more than decoding words for fluency; it involves making sense of text using a variety of appropriate strategies—a process that often confounds struggling readers. Fluency is an attribute of oral speech that for most requires practice using familiar text. The miscues that occur prior to the reader being able to read "fluently" actually point the reader toward becoming fluent. When the focus of fluency instruction is on repetitive practice aimed at speed, pace, and expression, students are not given opportunities to reflect on their reading habits and miscues. Fluency is expected in drama and the arts—when reading has been practiced. Miscues occur during "cold reads" of unfamiliar text to give us a window on the reading process.

Using RMA helps students better understand the reading process and become better, more confident readers. Moreover, the use of RMA to integrate content across the curriculum is powerful. Teachers will enjoy the opportunity to connect good children's literature, both fiction and nonfiction, to other content areas as they choose RMA reading selections. Through RMA conversations, readers will then begin to make connections between a variety of texts and content in authentic and meaningful ways that involve inquiry into their own understanding of the reading process situated in a variety of contexts both as individuals and collectively as a classroom community.

In summary, when readers examine their miscues and retellings, they look at the reasoning behind the miscue drawing from their intrinsic knowledge of language systems. Teachers who view miscues as evidence of the reader's attempts to construct meaning will never listen to a child read in the same way again.

2 RMA and the Theoretical Premises Involved

When you're trying to retell something, it's okay to say you're confused.

—Vicki

This chapter will do the following:

- Explain the theoretical framework for Retrospective Miscue Analysis (RMA)
- Explore the systems of language
- Connect miscue analysis to the systems of language

THEORETICAL FRAMEWORK FOR RMA

We have learned from our students that the success of RMA is grounded in the use of language, and language is one of the most accessible and useful teaching tools. In this chapter, we explain the theoretical underpinnings of RMA and the systems of language that aid in understanding the miscues readers make. One important premise behind RMA stems from Vygotsky's theory of the zone of proximal development (ZPD), the distance between what the child is able to do independently and the level of

SOURCE: This chapter was adapted from Moore & Gilles, 2005, with permission.

potential development—what the child is able to do under the guidance of an adult or a more capable peer (Vygotsky, 1978). In RMA, readers benefit from knowledgeable others and from social interaction leading to new understandings; this situation places the learner in an environment that validates the worth and potential of the reader. Learners are empowered to discuss the reading process by analyzing their own miscues and those of their peers in small, safe, collaborative learning groups facilitated by the teacher.

Second, understanding the reading process through features of language is important to miscue analysis and RMA because, as mentioned in Chapter 1, proficient and nonproficient readers all depend on the same process when reading: sampling, predicting, confirming, and correcting as needed. (More discussion about this process takes place in Chapter 3.) The difference in readers' success is due to how well they control their reading and understanding of language to construct meaning (Goodman & Marek, 1996). The reading process is tied closely to implicit knowledge and awareness of the systems of language.

SYSTEMS OF LANGUAGE

Knowing about the systems of language helps teachers understand the features readers use and those they do not use proficiently or ignore as they read. Analyzing how a reader uses the systems of language makes it easier for a teacher to build a reading instruction program that fits that reader's needs. The systems of language include the linguistic systems and the pragmatic systems. These systems work together as a student reads to provide meaning and context for decoding and understanding the text. The following are the subsystems that support the linguistic and pragmatic language systems.

Linguistic systems (language systems)

- semantic (meaning)
- syntactic (structure and grammar)
- graphophonic (sound-symbol)

Pragmatic systems ("language in use")

- context of situation
- background knowledge
- culture (Goodman, Watson, & Burke, 1987)

Connecting Miscue Analysis to the Systems of Language

Examining how a reader uses the linguistic systems gives teachers valuable information about how students use knowledge of how language works in their reading. This cueing system includes information about how the reader uses meaning, the structure of the sentence (grammar), and visual information.

Making meaning is the purpose of reading and is crucial to the process; thus, the *semantic* system is at the heart of the systems of language. For example, a beginning teacher early in the school year listened to each one of her fifth-grade students read to determine individual reading abilities. One child, Sofia, read the passage perfectly, using fairly good intonation and making no miscues. However, when the teacher asked her to retell the passage, Sofia replied, "No habla ingles!" Sofia could decode—sound out the words in the passage—but since her first language was Spanish and she only spent a few months each year in the United States, she had almost no understanding of what she read. Sofia was not an effective reader. Even though she read miscue-free, she was not constructing meaning while reading (Moore & Gilles, 2005). Teaching readers to always sound out the word and pay attention to the graphophonic system's features creates an over reliance on one system. For Sofia, proficiency in oral reading did not support her understanding of the text. This happens frequently with second language learners of English, particularly those whose native graphophonic structures are similar to those of English.

More typically, students who are not gaining meaning pronounce nonwords that may look like the text. When they read something that does not fit the meaning of the story and do not pause, a teacher can later ask, "Does that make sense?" or "Does that sound like language?" The first is an important question that relies on the semantic system, while the second relies on the syntactic system. Questions like these are asked during RMA, especially during the first few conversations to call attention to how language supports reading and vice versa.

All meaning is controlled within the structure of the language, the *syntax*, or *grammar*. Children come to school with an innate grammatical knowledge of English. They know that in the sentence, "John ran down the ______," the word in the blank has to be a word like *street* or *stairs* (nouns). It can't be *running* (verb) or some other part of speech. Readers use this innate knowledge as they read. Syntax includes the surface structures, "the relationships signaled by word endings, function words and word order" and also the deep structure, "the underlying relations among words of a sentence" (Weaver, 1980, p. 22). When readers take the surface structure and translate it into a more comfortable deep structure, they have used the syntactic system. For example, Watson (1996b, p. 17) reports this miscue:

minute
Stop. Wait a moment, Timber

The reader translated *moment* into a more comfortable structure, *minute* without changing the meaning. If readers make miscues that are nonwords but look like the text word and do not stop to correct, teachers can ask them the question, "Does that sound like language?" This question helps readers focus on the syntactic system.

Of course reading cannot happen without the printed symbols on the page, the *grapho-phonemes.* The letters, the white spaces between them, the font, the size of print, and so on, all give readers information about what the message might be; however, the more background readers have on the topic and the better predictions they make, the less they actually depend on the grapho-phonemes. In addition, it is possible to still read and interpret the text without reading every phoneme on the page.

Pragmatic systems

While the features of the linguistic systems are vitally important, the aspects of the *pragmatic systems* also can inform teachers. Pragmatic means language in use; the pragmatic system includes a reader's background experience, the context of situation, and the culture. The example that always resonates with Rita's college classes is this one: When you talk with you friends about last night's big party, you might not tell the story in the same way or with the same intonations or examples that you do when you explain to your grandmother about the same event. Here's another one: When telling your good friend you like her apartment, you might say, "Groovy crib, girlfriend," but in telling your professor she has a nice place, you might say something such as, "What a lovely home you have!" The light always comes on when preservice teachers hear these examples and many of their own emerge.

Context of situation refers to expectations of readers and intentions of authors (Watson, 1988). People form expectations based on past experiences. For example, children who have had read fairytales read to them expect that a new tale will begin "Once upon a time" and end "happily ever after." In their experiences with the fairytale genre, "once upon a time" has occurred without fail (Moore & Gilles, 2005). Discussing the structures students might expect in certain texts or genres can help them navigate the text more easily. If students know that science texts often are structured around specific vocabulary and explanations, they can make better decisions about reading the text more effectively.

Background of experience is crucial to making meaning. Readers bring their own background knowledge to reading and integrate it with the words on the page to create meaning; thus, the more background about the topic a reader has, the easier it will be to make logical predictions, monitor, and create appropriate meanings. Consider how you read something familiar. Is it easy? Now, think about something difficult. Is it more difficult and less enjoyable? When readers know little about the topic, the vocabulary becomes more problematic and predictions are less sure, thus helping students build background through prereading discussions about the illustrations, characters, language patterns, or story structure is essential to reading with meaning (Fountas & Pinnell, 1996).

A reader's *culture* surrounds all of the systems of language. Everything readers hear or say is filtered through their own language and cultural experiences. When passages of reading conflict with the reader's experiences, they are more difficult to read. Try reading a passage from one of the *Amelia Bedelia* books, replete with malapropisms and metaphors such as "under the weather" or "weeding the garden." The first simply does not make sense to someone from another language culture, and the second, in some grammars, might suggest adding weeds rather than taking them out! Imagine how speakers of other languages who live in the United States struggle with the cultural overtones of literature written by Americans! Everything we read is culture laden.

Readers use *all* of the linguistic and pragmatic features as they read. Dorothy Watson (1988) explains, "Within the complexly organized systems of language there are subsystems that work in concert to help humans organize their experiences and mediate meaning" (p. 5). All of these systems work together, not in isolation, to help readers construct meaning.

Is this only for English?

No, these linguistic systems are alive and well in all languages. Couple the understanding of reading strategies and systems, and you engage in a powerful knowledge of how to teach all readers to become proficient and especially acquire a sense of how English Language Learners (ELL) use the same strategies they used to learn to read in their first language as they do in their second. No matter how proficient ELLs may be in any language, the strategies and systems they need to learn and understand through authentic conversations and classroom work are the same.

REFLECTION

The reading strategies readers choose to use continually interact with the linguistic systems and subsystems. Analyzing how a reader uses the systems of language makes it easier for a teacher to build a reading instruction program that fits that reader's needs.

When students read, they sample from print and make predictions. Their predictions are based on their background, their culture, the situational context, and specific linguistic systems. Having background knowledge and connections about the text is critical to being able to successfully predict and ultimately comprehend what is being read. They use the letters, white spaces, and the shape of the word, as well as the structure of the sentence and the meaning of the word and/or the sentence, to help them predict the next structure. When they confirm, they again check the syntactic and semantic acceptability for the sentence. They then integrate the author's meaning with their own background of meaning and comprehend the text (Goodman, 1996).

Talking about the miscues of language and how they impact meaning or advancing the reading strategies used to navigate the text supports the development of critical literacy in all children regardless of ability or language history. Teachers who choose to raise the reader's awareness of the reading process through safe, informative, and interactive discussion about miscues demonstrate their commitment to valuing and empowering learners.

3 Connecting the Reading Process to Miscue Analysis

Maybe because she reads so fast she puts in words.

—Conrad, a third grader

This chapter will do the following:

- Explore the reading process
- Provide a quick overview of miscue analysis
- Examine the relationship between miscues and the reading process
- Demonstrate there is more than one kind of miscue

THE READING PROCESS

After extensive research, Kenneth Goodman (1984, 1994) developed a theory of the reading process. Goodman suggests that readers *sample* from text and *predict* the next feature or plot event in the text. Because language is redundant and predictable, efficient readers use what they need to make meaning instead of consciously processing every phoneme. They use their background information, predictions, and key visual information to make sense of the text.

To test sampling at work, discover how many vanity car license plates you can decipher correctly. Readers make meaning from sequences without vowels, like *I lv tski* (I love to ski), because they rely more on consonants than vowels for meaning (Weaver, Gillmeister-Krause, and Vento-Zogby, 1996, p. 33). Consonants are generally "constant" in sound features while vowels are chameleons, changing their sounds as they move from one linguistic environment to the next. Consider the unaccented second syllable of many words in English, which is called a *schwa* and sounds like "uh." It may be spelled with an *e* as in *basketball*, or an *i* as in *motivate*.

Most people are able to predict the next few words of any familiar text based on the meaning of the piece and the redundancy of language. Of course, the more familiar readers are with the topics, the easier this is to do. As readers continue in the text, they *confirm* the predictions they have made with the actual text. Then they *integrate* the meaning they have formed from their background experiences with the authors' meaning, thereby creating the meaning of the text (Goodman, 1984, 1994; Rosenblatt, 1938/1976). If readers fail to make meaning, they have the option to resample, rethink, repredict, and then integrate or to stop their reading. Readers who monitor their understanding know when they need to slow down, reread or repredict, but these are strategies that sometimes need to be taught to *striving* readers. Miscue analysis is a powerful procedure based on over 45 years of research on the reading process, linguistics, reader response, and cognitive psychology. For a more complete summary of the research, see Resource A.

QUICK OVERVIEW OF MISCUE ANALYSIS

Though a detailed discussion of miscue analysis procedures appears in Chapter 4, a quick overview here provides some context for readers with little background in miscue analysis. In miscue analysis, the teacher asks the student to read an unfamiliar text that has a beginning, middle, and end and is somewhat challenging. Vicki used literacy stations, further explained in Chapter 4, so that students could complete the readings and retellings independently. While word length of the reading varies, it usually takes a text of about 150 to 250 words to gather sufficient miscues but still not be so challenging the reader will give up. Be especially sensitive to English language learners (ELL) students who are just learning to read in English for whom the passage length may need to be modified.

Next, the teacher audiotapes the session then marks all of the reader's miscues on a typescript. (Resource B is an example of a marked typescript.) At the end of the reading, the teacher asks the student to retell the story to gain an overall sense of the student's understanding. Often, a retelling protocol is used that assigns points for plot development, characters, setting, and theme. See Resource C for an example; Resource D is an example for expository text.

After the session, the teacher checks the markings for accuracy and codes each of the miscues to determine the relationship of the miscues to the systems of language. For example, is the miscue one of substitution and if so, is it semantically acceptable? And is there a noticeable pattern of substitutions of certain words that may be graphophonically similar? A common miscue is *the* for *they*. Sometimes readers "hang on" to the same miscue for some time then realize what they are reading is not making sense and change it. *Sing* substituted for *sign* is one that comes to mind.

Taking a close look at the miscues and the retelling helps the teacher understand the strategies the reader used or ignored. Questions to consider as you analyze the miscues and retelling include the following:

1. Did the reader decode slowly and miss the meaning of the story?
2. Did the reader mistake one letter for another and guess, thus suggesting over dependence on graphic information?
3. Did the reader supply words that fit the grammar of the sentence but were not meaningful, thereby using the syntax of the sentence but not the semantics?

Analyzing the results of the miscues helps the teacher better understand how students read and what might be done to help them be more efficient and effective readers. Figure 3.1 provides a quick guide to miscue analysis procedures leading to RMA.

Figure 3.1 Quick Guide to Miscue Analysis

1. Select texts to use for miscue analysis and get equipment ready.
2. Create typescript for the reader. Either type one or photocopy and enlarge.
3. Make your reader comfortable and give the instructions. Don't forget to turn on the tape recorder.
4. Mark the typescript as the reader reads.
5. Conduct the retelling. Include the aided retelling to get as much information as possible.
6. Prepare the RMA Organizer for the RMA conversation.
7. Plan instructional strategies to support the individual strengths and needs of the reader.

THE RELATIONSHIP OF MISCUES TO THE READING PROCESS

A miscue is a reader's variation from print—that is, anything the reader says that does not exactly match the text. The goal of miscue analysis is to "describe, explain, and evaluate a reader's control or ownership of the [reading] process" (Goodman, Watson, & Burke, 1987, p. 3). In miscue analysis teachers and/or researchers listen to a student read an unfamiliar passage of narrative or expository text, mark the unexpected responses (miscues), and then code and analyze them to find patterns in the student's reading behavior grounding their analysis in what they find the reader knows about the use of language.

Miscue analysis is based on two important ideas: (1) everyone miscues (deviates from the written text), and (2) miscues do not equal errors (Watson, 1996a). Miscues include a continuum of unexpected responses, from those that do not change the meaning of the text to those that change the meaning considerably. It is important to remember that no miscue is without meaning. Each one reveals the reader's interpretation of text and understanding of language. All people miscue. One of our colleagues described a miscue that is reminiscent of those we all make. Driving home from work one day a long time after lunch, she stopped for a passing train. The train had "Chesapeake" painted on the side but our colleague uttered "cheesecake" aloud then laughed at her own miscue. Her hunger had colored her perceptions and caused a miscue. Miscues are a part of our daily language use and provide us with the chance to metacognitively examine our own awareness of how we interpret the world.

Formal meetings where minutes are read or a scripted procedure is followed are usually replete with miscues as the reader translates the text into language that is a bit more comfortable or natural. Proficient readers often substitute *a* for *the* or move text around slightly. In addition, we have all heard newscasts during which the reader might not anticipate upcoming punctuation in the script. Often, as soon as it's spoken, the reader self-corrects because of knowledge of language. When children are encouraged to treat reading as a meaning-making process rather than a subject to study, they become more efficient and effective readers, using their knowledge of language and language systems to construct meaning.

Is It Important to Fix Every Miscue?

Only miscues that significantly interfere with meaning need to be fixed, but they are still as important to discuss as "smart" miscues because they demonstrate how the mind works while reading. Moreover, readers need to know it's quite all right to substitute or skip words since that's what all readers do. In miscue analysis, the foundation for RMA, the reader's miscues are valued because their patterns tell us what is going on in the mind of the reader during the reading process. If we correct the miscues, we won't see miscue patterns and a valuable source of information about the reader is lost.

More Than One Kind of Miscue

Just as there are many nuances of linguistic meaning, there are different kinds of miscues. Goodman and Marek (1996) call miscues that do not change the meaning *high quality miscues*, while those that do change the meaning are *low quality*. For example, consider the following:

to

1005 when you go into a cave in June or July, be sure to look for baby

The reader substitutes *to* for *into*. Working with students we have found the terms *high level* and *low level* are easily understood. Because the miscue does not change the meaning considerably, we call it a high level miscue (Moore & Gilles, 2005). Consider this second example by Phoenix (a third grader from Vicki's classroom):

creeps

502 its insect prey, it slowly crept closer.

Phoenix substituted *creeps* for *crept*, a past-tense form of creep that he has possibly heard before but perhaps not seen in print. Phoenix's substitution did not change the meaning; therefore, it is considered another high level miscue.

REFLECTION

In this chapter, we have presented a quick overview of miscue analysis, especially for those readers who may not be familiar with this approach to reading assessment and instruction. Teachers often comment that after conducting miscue analyses with just a few readers, they never listen to children or adults read in the same way again. Miscue analysis transforms our thinking about reading as a process supported by developing linguistic skills and the prior knowledge each reader brings to the reading event. Analyzing the reader's miscues is the first step in helping the reader understand there is meaning behind each miscue. This makes how children develop as readers and consumers of language more transparent and meaningful to the reader and the teacher.

Chapter 4 will explain how to conduct miscue analysis and suggest procedures for analyzing and storing the miscue data for RMA when children are paired with other readers to interactively discuss their miscues of language and meaning.

4 Marking and Coding Miscues for RMA

Simplifying the Process for Classroom Teachers

I've wanted to try RMA for some time, but the miscue analysis scares me a little.

—Vicki, a fifth-grade classroom teacher

This chapter will do the following:

- Provide steps in conducting miscue analyses
- Provide a guide for marking miscues
- Suggest procedures for collecting and storing miscue data

DEMYSTIFYING THE MISCUE CODING PROCESS

Marking and coding miscues are necessary for Retrospective Miscue Analysis (RMA) conversations, but too often teachers are bogged down in the miscue analysis process. They fail to understand the rationale behind the coding, which simply is to identify enough miscues in addition to information from the student retelling of the text to sustain meaningful RMA conversations.

Steps in Conducting the Miscue Analysis

The student reads aloud from an unfamiliar, challenging text of about 150 to 250 words (for elementary students) while the teacher listens to and marks the miscues defined as the unexpected responses to text in the oral reading. By *challenging*, we mean a text that is approximately one reading level above the reader's instructional level. Number of words depends largely on the reader's ability and teacher's best judgment. The text should be a "whole" text not word lists or isolated sentences so the readers is provided with a sense of story or organizational framework.

Prior to the readings, Vicki tells the readers that they will read without help or interruptions, and when they have finished reading, they will be asked to tell as much about their reading as they remember. The teacher may prefer that children audiotape their readings independently in a classroom workstation so that she might mark them later, thus saving time and effort. This first session is called *conducting a miscue analysis.* (An example of one of the marked texts referred to in this book is located as Resource B.)

Note that the miscue analysis text is numbered in the left-hand margin so that identifying the miscue during RMA discussions is easy for students and teachers (see Resource E). During RMA, students simply refer to the line where the miscue occurred. For instance, Elizabeth might say, "On line 504, I left a word out." Here's a helpful tip: Vicki marked each text with a different set of numbers so that it was easier for her own recordkeeping. The first text read was marked with 100s, the second with 200s, and so on. She also enlarged the text so that it was easier for students to read and easier for her to have space to mark the miscues.

Markings of miscues fall into several categories: repetitions, omissions (words that the student deletes or does not read), insertions (additions to the text), and substitutions (another word is substituted for the one in the text). Patterns in miscues will begin to emerge such as repetitions serving as a reading placeholder. In addition, self-corrections, dialect, and transposed words are marked. Notes can be made about when students struggle with proper nouns within the text or words that are difficult for them (often these are words that students have never heard before or have never seen in print).Vicki also marks when students ignore or insert punctuation because an RMA discussion around such miscues can be far more powerful than any mini-lesson intentionally planned for and taught. Figure 4.1 provides a guide to miscue marking for teachers.

Following the reading, the student gives an oral summary of the text, called a *retelling* in which the reader is instructed to recall as much information from the text as possible without looking back. Conducting a retelling reinforces the idea that reading is for meaning. The teacher may use a retelling protocol like those found in Resources C and D.

Figure 4.1 Miscue Marking Guide

Omissions: When a word is left out, it will be circled. He (ate) slowly.

quickly
Insertions: When a word is added, use a carat to mark it. She ^ ran home.

®
Repetitions: When a word is repeated, use a circled *R* to mark it. Mary Mary swam

Reversals: When words are reversed, use lines to mark it. **to** **remember**

Substitutions: When a word is substituted for another, it is written above the text. **Him**
her

Self-corrections: When a word(s) are corrected after a miscue, use a circled *C* to mark it.

©
hit
Jason hung the ball.

Dialect: When a word or phrase pronunciation may be attributed to dialect, a *D* is written above the word.

D
larned
learned

Next, the teacher transfers the miscues and a summary of the retelling to a Simplified Miscue Organizer (Moore & Gilles, 2005) included as a reproducible in Resource G. While some teachers prefer to use a more detailed organizer (see Moore & Gilles, 2005) for classroom research purposes, we find the simplified version more user friendly for teachers and students. Copies of the Simplified Miscue Organizer are then made for the RMA group members. The process of transcribing miscues and keeping track of patterns through a miscue organizer takes only minutes once a teacher begins incorporating the procedure into a classroom literacy block.

A Frequently Asked Question: How to Select Text for Miscue Readings?

We believe it is important that the text be somewhat challenging, allowing at least a few miscues but not so difficult that the number of miscues interferes with the student's ability to comprehend and conduct a retelling.

For example, in gathering miscues for one RMA group to discuss, Vicki selected a text about Rosa Parks (Wilson, 2001) for each group member to read that was probably too difficult—her proficient readers were producing far more miscues than normal. The students' readings on audiotapes were noticeably halting and far less fluent, but the students were still able to retell with success. Some of that success can be credited to these students' overall ability to continually confirm for meaning (a skill they have mastered), but largely their ability to comprehend this particular text was due to having background knowledge about Rosa Parks, segregation, and civil rights. Another group of less skilled readers would not have been so successful at comprehending a passage this far above their reading level. It is absolutely critical that the teacher take into account the skills of the readers, their ability to apply strategies they already know, and the type of text being presented to the students.

A GUIDE FOR MARKING MISCUES

Learning to mark miscues takes a little time and practice. Don't worry about getting the markings exactly correct each time, and develop your own shorthand to help you memorize and learn the markings. After some practice, teachers naturally learn to use the markings much like the editing markings we use to guide student writings.

The following are examples of marked miscues from the students in Vicki's classroom and possible ways to address the miscues during RMA sessions, or if deemed appropriate, follow-up lessons during guided reading or whole class instruction.

Omissions

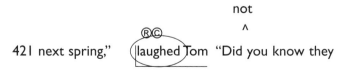

not
^
®©
421 next spring," laughed Tom "Did you know they

Here Scott omitted the word *laughed* and ignored the period after *Tom*. Instead, he spoke as if the sentence read, "Tom did not you know they. . . ." The ® © denotes that Scott repeated, and when he did, he self-corrected his miscues.

The omission that Scott made does not affect the meaning of the text, thus a smart miscue. The repetition and self-correction present an opportunity to praise Scott for self-monitoring when he is reading and noting that repeating and self-correcting help the reader understand the text. A teacher noticing lots of miscues around punctuation could plan mini-lessons for those students experiencing difficulties with this skill. Later, during RMA, a teacher in tune with these kinds of miscues may target the group of students needing assistance while other students do not need instruction around this skill.

Insertions

Autumn's insertion of the word *sat* in the following example makes sense. The sentence remains syntactically correct, and for a third-grade student, probably sounds better than what was originally written. In an RMA discussion, we would call this a smart miscue.

111 different in Louis's day. The boys sat on one

sat
^

112 side of the room, the girls on the other. The

Substitutions

When marking substitutions, write the substituted word above the word in the text that the reader miscues on. Sometimes a miscue occurs in a sentence, and even though the miscue isn't corrected, the sentence, as read, is syntactically correct. Here is an example of this occurring while Autumn was reading:

120 he could. He had to. He could not read. He

to
^

121 had to listen and remember. It was the only

Here is another substitution miscue, this time from Phoenix. While the miscue seems syntactically correct, it affects Phoenix's retelling.

507 rush into its legs. Did you ever pour water into a balloon and see it

explode
^

508 expand?

When Phoenix conducts his retelling, he states, "Its legs [a spider] are kind of like a balloon, and then it explodes." Vicki makes a note on the Retelling Guide for Expository Text (see Resource D), "Incorrect information: Read the word *expands* as *explodes* in the text." Another substitution from Bastian in this example, affects the meaning of the text:

206 predator. It is a big

207 coyote! Prairie Dog

from
^
208 dives for a burrow.

This miscue would lead the reader to think that when a prairie dog encounters a predator, it might leave its burrow rather than dive for safety. During RMA, a discussion could ensue about how similar the words *from* and *for* appear, but the miscue is only "okay" because it affected the understanding of the text.

Repetitions

Repetitions are noted by making an *L* shape around the portion of the text that is repeated along with an ® marking, like so:

®
726 boarded a public bus, sat down in a seat, and began a

Repetitions may be viewed as placeholders in miscue analysis or as evidence the reader is confirming meaning or struggling with it. They are not considered miscues. Some readers are holding their place while quickly looking back, and others repeat when they have looked too far ahead and are "gaining their bearings" before they continue to read again. Occasionally, a student repeats so often that it becomes a habit interfering with fluency. For example, Katie was in Vicki's class for fourth grade and looped with her to fifth. She had excellent comprehension skills and successfully read and enjoyed books above grade level. She frequently bought books for the classroom because she knew Vicki and classmates would appreciate and read them.

When Katie read aloud, she repeated so often that it was difficult to focus on the context of the text. Vicki avoided putting her into situations where she was asked to read in front of others. She asked Katie to be one of four students to engage in a collaborative RMA process to work on her reading skills, specifically repeating while reading. In a conversation between Vicki and Katie, it became clear that she knew what caused her compromised fluency when Katie stated she became nervous when she had to read aloud.

Katie was very anxious during her first audio-taped session. She repeated 22 times during the reading. During the RMA discussion of her tape, she noted how many times she had repeated. After that, Katie's repetitions diminished by half and continued to decline with each subsequent read. Eventually, she was able to read aloud in class and fluently perform in Reader's Theater with such expression her peers applauded her "performance."

Reversals

A reversal is marked in this way:

Tom
^
421 next spring," laughed Tom. "Did you know they

In this example, David reversed *laughed* and *Tom* but then inserted *Tom* in front of the next sentence. So the miscues make sense and are deemed smart miscues.

Dealing With Proper Nouns

Many times, proper nouns get in the students' way when they are reading text. Sometimes it affects meaning, and sometimes it does not. If the proper noun is a person's name in narrative text, it may not make a difference how the name is read. However, in the miscue that follows, Conrad has miscued the name of a city that is critical information for understanding how civil rights played out in the South.

®© Montchipee
701 On a crisp, cool day in Montgomery, Alabama,

This miscue provided an opportunity for Vicki to talk about Montgomery, Alabama, during social studies. Note that Vicki often chose RMA text that was integrated with what students were studying in other content areas.

Words That Are Difficult

Difficult words for students to decode and pronounce present unique opportunities to discuss vocabulary. In the example that follows, the word is made even more complicated for Kathie to read because it is hyphenated.

ig-
integrate
704 move to the rear of the bus. Parks' actions ig-

nitted
705 nited a city bus boycott in Montgomery, a year-

A long discussion ensues about hyphenated words. The students come to the understanding that as they become more competent and read more challenging texts, they will encounter new conventions that may test them as readers but ultimately assist them in mastering new skills.

Just for Practice

Teachers may find Resource E, a practice reproducible text for coding, helpful when practicing miscue marking. Copyright laws allow one copy per text for instructional purposes. An example of the same text with miscue markings is located as Resource B. Those who are new to miscue might form pairs, with one reading the text as marked while the other practices marking miscues and conduct a retelling using the Retelling Guide for Expository Text in Resource D. Then review for marking accuracy with the marked text in Resource B, then switch roles. Follow up this practice by asking questions about the miscues and retelling just as you would if you were members of an RMA group.

COLLECTING AND STORING THE MISCUE DATA

We have found that organizing carefully for collecting miscue data is key to successful implementation of classroom RMA. Find ways of collecting data, like learning stations, that may already exist in your classroom. Allowing students to be the data collectors (in this case, recording their own reading and retelling) empowers them to have increased ownership in the process. A short amount of training time is all that is required.

Setting Up Literacy Stations

Set up a place or places in your classroom with a tape recorder; provide each student's folder with a tape and unmarked typescript. You may wish to put more than one typescript in the folder in numerical sequence after the first time or two, but keep it simple in the beginning. Maintain and post a list of who is to record his or her reading on which date on the board or a classroom chart just as you would any other ongoing assignment or guided reading rotation. Check the stations periodically to be sure the students are actually taping the readings, as sometimes mechanical problems may occur resulting in no recording taking place.

The photograph in Figure 4.2 demonstrates how the audiotaping station might look in a typical classroom setting.

Figure 4.2 Audiotaping Literacy Station

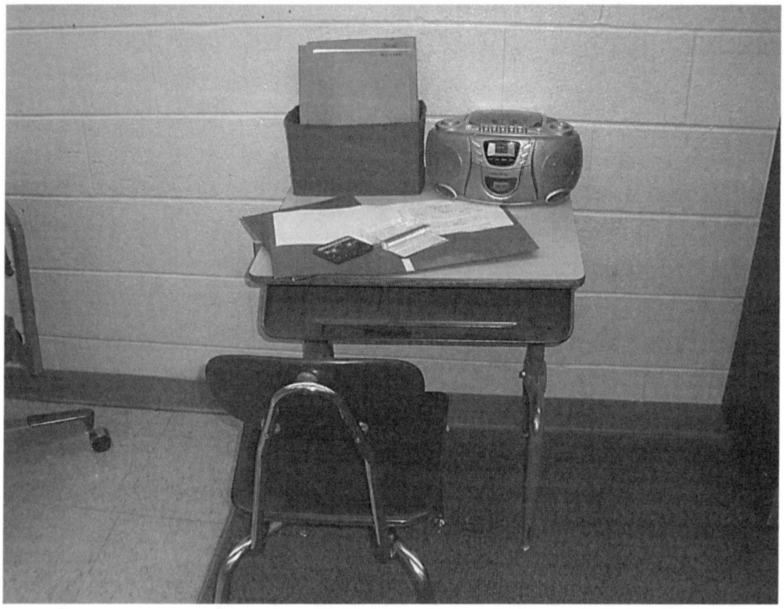

It is most important to find out what miscues the readers makes and if they change the meaning of the text. During the miscue reading, tell the readers they are to read as though they were on their own. One of the reasons we believe in having audiotaping stations is that there is no opportunity to look to the teacher for help. In miscue analysis, the goal is for the reader to be independent—to do one's own work so that the reader owns what is taken to the RMA conversation.

More on Data Collection and Storage

The data collection process must work for the teacher. In Vicki's case, a three-ring binder was utilized because it was easy to retrieve information when meeting with parents or colleagues about students' progress in reading. Some teachers may prefer individual student folders kept in a filing cabinet. Each page of text (enlarged and lines numbered in the left-hand margin) she used to collect miscues was included in this section. It is helpful to note the text title, the author's name, and the level of the text used with students (sometimes this is an approximation based on teacher experiences with text as all text used is not "leveled" in the literal meaning of the word).

In Chapter 5, we will discuss how to organize the classroom for RMA in detail and continue to elaborate on the data collection and storage process.

REFLECTION

The examples from Vicki's classroom clearly indicate that coding miscues to prepare for RMA is not unwieldy and neither is the data collection and storage design. Miscue analysis represents a thoughtful, careful approach to understanding the meaning behind the reader's miscue in a way that makes sense to both the reader and the teacher. And it is a data gathering, preparatory process for the next step, which is the RMA discussion. Once you have conducted a few miscue analyses and perhaps modified the miscue organizer to best fit your teaching style and classroom needs, then it becomes a seamless part of how you begin to assess and interpret the literacy learning of each child in your classroom. The time spent transcribing and recording data is minimal, and the data will change the teacher's view of each reader in the classroom.

5 Organizing the Classroom for RMA

I knew what it means, but I couldn't pronounce it.

—Conrad, a third grader

This chapter will do the following:

- Provide rationale for using Retrospective Miscue Analysis (RMA) with an entire class of readers
- Introduce RMA as a two-part process
- Provide step-by-step suggestions for implementing RMA into the literacy curriculum
- Emphasize the importance of retelling during RMA

RATIONALE FOR INVOLVING THE ENTIRE CLASS IN RMA

Vicki practiced RMA with her fourth- and fifth-grade students two years before she moved to a third-grade classroom. You may recall from the introduction to this book that it was with her fifth-grade class that Vicki first began thinking about how to implement RMA in the classroom and find a way to share the outcomes of RMA conversations with the entire class. With the younger children, she built on her prior experiences in using RMA over an extended period of time with struggling readers. She decided to try RMA with the entire classroom as an alternative approach to teaching reading, later using Socratic Circles as a way of having the entire class benefit from what was being learned in each of the RMA groups. (In Chapter 9, we more fully explain how to use Socratic Circles with RMA.)

The most important thing to remember about RMA is that it identifies and builds on student strengths not weaknesses, which for some educators and parents represents a paradigm shift. Reading "errors" are referred to as miscues not "mistakes" because every miscue has meaning. Every miscue reveals something about what the readers are thinking or how they are processing text during reading (Davenport, 2002; Wilde, 2000). These revelations become the fuel for discussion within the RMA group and provide the reader, peers, and teacher with information inaccessible by other small group-facilitated reading means. The teacher looks for patterns of miscues to better inform instructional decisions in reading and across the curriculum.

Another important concept to remember as one plans for RMA is that miscue analysis and RMA are built upon the use of the whole—the whole story, the whole sentence, the whole headline, and so on. Words and meaning are not taken out of the context of the whole making it easier for readers to understand the reading process.

And finally, RMA is really all about building trust among readers—trust that carries over into all aspects of the classroom day. Carefully explaining the process and the important responsibilities associated with the reading discussions lays critical groundwork for establishing communities of readers who trust and learn from one another.

In this chapter we will show how the process of RMA easily adapts to an elementary classroom setting. RMA requires no special resources other than appropriate reading materials and a tape recorder. More current technology resources, such as an iPod, may be available in many schools. Recently, Vicki wrote, submitted, and received monies from a district technology grant for current technological equipment—a digital video camera—for use with RMA groups. While not yet tested, we believe that a video of RMA groups in progress would be a powerful, new way to discuss reading behaviors with students, teachers, and parents.

RMA: A SIMPLE AND EFFECTIVE TWO-PART PROCESS

The following provides an overview of how miscue analysis and RMA connect as supporting processes.

Part 1: Preparing for RMA Through Miscue Analysis

This first step toward preparing for RMA conversations is the miscue analysis. While the kinds of texts and length may differ from classroom to classroom, the process is the same: the reader reads from text that represents a whole (not single sentences or word lists that have no meaningful connection) then the teacher analyzes the miscues and writes them on a miscue organizer using our suggested protocol or one she develops. In developing your own miscue organizer or modifying the one found in Resource G, it is important to include the line of the text and whether or not the miscue changed the meaning of the sentence in which it was read. For an alternative, the teacher may wish to sort the kinds of miscues that were made to establish a greater sense of linguistic patterns. For example, how many meaningful substitutions were made, or is the omission of a word a common reading behavior for the student? We suggest starting simple with the organizer we present and later, as you become more comfortable with the process, add features to the template that may tell you more about the reader. It is also important to fill out a retelling guide to be stored with all of the reader's data (see Resources C and D) in order to know if the reader actually comprehended the story and the kinds of comprehension patterns that may emerge such as greater comprehension of nonfiction versus fiction text. Then, note one or two things that might be discussed during RMA on the miscue organizer.

Remember, the miscues are being collected in order for the reader and that reader's group members to provide information about the rationale behind the miscues so waiting for the explanation is often the most informative path. Here's an example of where it's valuable to wait: One reader read *security* in place of *secretary*. When asked about the miscue during RMA, he explained that he knew the word was *secretary* but that the school secretary is kind of "in charge, like a security guard." His explanation suggests a high level miscue took place (Moore & Gilles, 2005).

Part 2: RMA Discussion

The second part of the process is the RMA discussion, which essentially is a conversation between and among readers with the teacher gradually taking a less prominent role. The group members are handed their RMA organizers—one for each reader they will listen to that day. One person is in charge of running the tape player, and each time there is a miscue of interest to discuss, the player is stopped and the conversation begins with the reader being invited to first provide the rationale behind the miscue. The group then comments or helps the reader figure out thoughts that may have provoked the miscue. Most of the time the student whose turn it is to discuss miscues also chooses to operate the tape recorder (however, there were those students not quite adept at operating the equipment and then this task was shared in a respectful way). This allows the student to stop and begin the tape again after his or her self-selected miscue had been discussed within the group. Flexible ability grouping works well for RMA, although as we have learned, the conversations from all the groups are uniquely rich.

The teacher may record or videotape the RMA session or simply take observation notes as she moves from one group to another. Having an instructional assistant or parent volunteer is helpful when all groups are participating in individual discussions. Another approach is to pre-assign dates and times for each discussion group to meet. On some days, the rest of the class may form an outer circle and listen using Socratic Circle method or simply have other work to complete.

STEP-BY-STEP IMPLEMENTATION OF RMA

We are now ready to explain how a teacher can organize for RMA. While we have discovered our own process, we encourage teachers to find their own way and make changes that are appropriate to the needs, abilities, and perceptions of their students. The following step by step process explains how teachers might organize for RMA discussion groups. It is by no means a scripted formula, and teachers are encouraged to find ways of implementing RMA into their classroom reading programs where they think it fits the best. The following steps may easily be mini-lessons introduced over the course of a week or as long as it takes for the children and the teacher to become comfortable with the process.

Step 1: Unraveling the Code

Implementing RMA begins with unraveling the meaning of Retrospective Miscue Analysis: three seemingly complicated, puzzling words, not just to teachers but to students and parents as well. If the process is to be successful, then the language of the strategy must be learned. Begin the process by writing the three words on a piece of chart paper displayed on a classroom easel: take each word apart and talk about each of the words, inviting students to figure out what parts of the words they already know, what parts are unfamiliar to them, and then to offer explanations of what they think each word means and how they fit together as a whole.

For example, Vicki's students in math and science activities had heard of the word *retro*, and they articulated ideas about what *analysis* might mean. It did not take long for the students to understand they were about to explore something very important and "grown-up." And it did not take them long to develop their own definition of RMA. It is important that once established, the teacher writes the definition for RMA that the students settle on in a prominent place in the classroom. This allows the children to "own" the process and helps set the stage for using RMA across the curriculum, not limiting the strategies of RMA only to reading groups. When adults have asked Vicki what she is writing about [for the purposes of this book], they have a blank look on their face until they begin to think of each of the words independently. It is not long before they too, understand the meaning of RMA.

While it may be tempting to find another more condensed term for RMA, we have found that students like to unravel the meaning then simply refer to the process later as *RMA*. In addition, we have found that teaching the term actually assists in setting the groundwork for small group RMA conversations as we discuss how we might solve the meaning as a group. Discussion of the core terminology of miscue and RMA also provides the perfect opportunity for teachers to begin to discuss not only what a miscue is but also the different language systems that support the reading process of sampling, predicting, and confirming. Since the term *retrospective miscue analysis* is a whole and meaningful unit, the prospects for teaching children about language and miscues using this term are myriad.

Step 2: Understanding the Purpose

Next, explain to students that miscues are unexpected responses to written text based on some prior knowledge and give them plenty of examples. Be sure to emphasize that miscues are not "mistakes" that are "bad." And if we think about the reasons behind our miscues, it helps us learn more about our strengths and weaknesses as readers. Then create a chart paper poster with a list of the kinds of miscues that may be noted and discussed during RMA conversations. Start off simply by listing those miscues students will readily understand: *repetitions, substitutions, reversals,* and *omissions.* Point out to students that two of the words, *repetitions* and *reversals,* have a connection to math, and they will correctly identify what these might mean in reading. It is helpful to demonstrate the meaning of each by reading from text and purposefully making miscues. Resource F (Focusing on Miscues) is a student-friendly version of miscue markings to be shared with students either on a chart paper poster on in the RMA folders.

Students will quickly begin commenting, "Oh, I've done that before!" or "I do that when I read." A critical piece for students seemed to be acknowledgement by the teacher that *everyone* miscues, not just students learning to read and understand text. Equally important was Vicki's statement to the students that she miscues too. List an example of each type of miscue, clearly labeled, on chart paper that may later be displayed in the room.

This is also a useful process for ELL children who often assume that native English speakers may not or should not make miscues. Try to involve your ELL students by showing miscues that might be made in their birth language, either with their help, help from another bilingual student, help from a bilingual assistant, or from another teacher. Including the nuances of more than one language in RMA raises cultural and linguistic awareness in authentic, affirming, and meaningful ways. If a classroom is comprised of students who predominantly speak a language other than English and the teacher speaks only English, then you might use the RMA process to explore both the teachers' miscues and those of the students depending on the language(s) in use. Be sure to post the directions for RMA in *all* the languages spoken in your classroom, enlisting resources to have them translated and read aloud to the children.

Step 3: Developing an Understanding of Smart and Okay Miscues

Next, begin to help the reader understand the reading process. Discuss the difference between a "smart" miscue and an "okay" miscue—the difference between a miscue that makes some sense and does not significantly change meaning and a miscue that somewhat alters the meaning of the text but serves as a "placeholder" that allows the reader to keep on reading (Moore & Gilles, 2005). Okay miscues usually share some graphic or phonemic features of the word in the text and are often corrected by the reader as they continue to construct meaning. An example of a smart miscue would be reading *mom* for *mother*. An example of an okay miscue might be reading *sing* for *sign* but eventually realizing the word is *sign* based on other words encountered. Give students some examples of each, put them into mixed ability groups, and have them decide which are smart miscues and which might be okay miscues, providing reasons for their decisions. Talk about differences of opinion and validate the students' ideas and attempts. This presents yet another teachable moment for reinforcing the steps in the reading process: sampling, predicting, and confirming and what we know about language that cues us to make either smart or okay miscues.

As discussions unfolded during the RMA process, Vicki was often surprised that students had a clear reason for their miscue and justified the miscue as smart or okay in a way she had never thought about. For example, when a student miscued . . . *let them sail* for *let him sail*, the group discussed the miscue "sounding right" because there is more than one person on a ship. When Vicki asked the students how they know about this, one student pointed out the different jobs on a ship—knowledge about this stemming from a previous guided reading text. Another group member responded with a connection to a popular movie and justification for the miscue: "In *Pirates of the Caribbean,* tons of people were on the ship, so I think it's a smart miscue." We have noticed that readers quickly begin to use the language of okay and smart miscues to guide conversations. These are safe, nonjudgmental terms that promote thoughtful thinking and eliminate the idea that miscues are errors.

In another example, Autumn explained Kathie's miscue. Kathie left out the words *the* and *long* reading the sentence as follows, "At times they had to tow [the] boats, using [long] ropes . . . ." Autumn elaborates, "Those are omissions. They are smart miscues. On line 313 she said *brushed* instead of *brush.* It happened a long time ago, so it is past tense."

Again, the teacher can chart some examples of *smart* and *okay* miscues and post these in a prominent place in the classroom so as RMA conversations begin, students may refer to definitions as well as to established examples to facilitate discussions. This kind of thoughtful approach also helps students see the purpose in the RMA discussions.

Here's another example of readers identifying an okay miscue and the rationale behind it. Kathie is the reader. The tape plays for a few minutes then Nellie stops it to discuss Kathie's miscue, which doesn't change the meaning but might be syntactically confusing.

Nellie: On line 615, she said, "a hole into hide."

Vicki: Let me read it to you the way she read it and see if it's a smart or an okay miscue. "Sometimes the sea urchin utilizes its spines to scrape a hole into hide."

All: (Very seriously) It's an okay miscue.

Vicki: Do you ever read ahead? What did she do?

Nellie: She took the *in* and put it here instead of here, then she forgot it. But it makes sense.

Close the discussion by reminding students when miscues occur, they mean something; therefore, they are not errors or mistakes. An experience, prior knowledge, a strong reliance on graphophonic cues, a misconception—something logically triggered the miscue. One of the common approaches to teaching reading used by many reading programs is showing readers how to make connections to text drawing on life experiences or knowledge of other texts. This is important to introduce in a mini-lesson prior to RMA and to reinforce during RMA retellings as well as during other reading activities to better assist readers in more effectively and efficiently monitoring for meaning.

In addition, Vicki and the students found it helpful to agree to always avoid the word *mistake* when they worked together in RMA groups, instead using the term *miscue* to talk about their readings. And as it turned out, the students rarely slipped and referred to mistakes during their RMA sessions. More often than not, it was Vicki who slipped, and students who reminded her!

Step 4: Conducting Retellings

If you recall from earlier chapters, the reader will not only be recording oral reading but will also provide a short retelling of the text. Explain that the readers will not only be examining their oral reading miscues but will also be "retelling" as much as they can remember about the text into the tape recorder when they finished reading without looking back.

Readers new to RMA may not fully understand what is expected of them during the retelling. It is helpful to discuss what constitutes a "quality" retelling as you model some examples for the class. You might use an interactive reading activity such as a shared book experience in which the teacher conducts a Think Aloud. During this strategy the teacher, as reader, models what she is thinking while reading (Vacca & Vacca, 2007). (More about Think Alouds appears in Chapter 8, detailing their importance and showing how readers utilize the strategy in a classroom discussion.) The student only reads the passage once into the tape recorder then conducts the retelling. Conversely, during the RMA conversation, readers are encouraged to reread the text and search for missing details. Once a student within an RMA group is able to articulate a particularly strong retelling, each of the other students understands exactly what a quality retelling sounds like providing proof that the peer teaching and learning process underscoring RMA is powerful.

Step 5: Organizing for RMA

Following the initial orientation to the language of RMA and the rationale behind it, the students are now ready to learn how to organize for RMA. They will receive their RMA folders and learn about the operation of the cassette recorder so recording of miscues and retelling of text by each child can begin. The teacher should identify flexible ability reading groups or those that will rotate based on progress and/or need of the readers. Students are assigned to groups of no more than five readers. It is helpful to prepare some sort of group reading activity such as listening to a story and retelling it as a group to assist the group members in beginning to work together.

GROUPING FOR RMA

Grouping for RMA is done in a careful, thoughtful manner. The most critical thing you can do when grouping for RMA is think about the strengths each student can bring to a larger group of students and how those strengths will scaffold the learning taking place within the group. For example, in the striving group of readers, Vicki placed readers together that are not often "heard" in other classroom discussions so that they could find their voices about the competencies they do have related to reading skills. In particular, Abigail and Jennie have lots of insightful advice to offer a group of readers that struggle with saying the words but often have good comprehension. Their reflective, constructive comments build confidence in the other readers in the group.

In the group of developing readers, two sensitive students, Ron and Elizabeth, are particularly careful about how they craft their sentences responding to other students. This is in contrast to Phoenix who tends to "tell it like it is!" The balance achieved by grouping these students together created a congenial group that could always be counted on for thought-provoking comments about the reading that takes place. Conversations were always lively and capitalized on every student's strengths.

The proficient group of readers initially struggled with conversation flow (a problem the other striving and developing groups never experienced). Vicki believes this may have occurred because they all thought of themselves as competent readers, but when miscues were examined, they realized that even a skilled, confident reader will read text differently than printed. She thinks too that they may have viewed these as "mistakes" initially and had to be convinced that all readers miscue for important reasons.

While we do assign readers to flexible ability groups for RMA, they are grouped primarily by the kinds of strategies they use in reading and those they want or need to work on—not on test scores. The basis of the group format is not about ability as much as it is about the students' knowledge and effective application of reading strategies related primarily to vocabulary and comprehension. This approach is defined quite well in the work of Sharon Taberski (2000, 2008), a classroom teacher who believes as we do in the power of talking about text and children's shared understandings of learning. Chapters 10 through 12 highlight the kinds of strategies each of the groups pursued.

The group members are given a copy of the coded text to follow as they listen to the taped reading of each group member. As they listen, the reader is given the first opportunity to stop the tape to discuss a miscue or the retelling with group members. Group members may then stop the tape to point out or question aspects of the reader's thinking while reading as with the example of Elizabeth given earlier. In essence, the reader is encouraged first to examine miscues to determine whether or not they changed the meaning of the text and second to decide what strategies might be most effective in helping monitor for meaning. Participants then help one another understand the reasoning behind the miscue or discuss details from the retelling. The teacher is there to guide the group with the goal of eventually relinquishing her role as facilitator. She may move from one RMA group to another if more than one RMA group is meeting. The way RMA is scheduled is entirely up to the teacher but can be rotated similarly to guided reading groups.

The fundamental questions asked by both teachers and readers during RMA conversations follow:

1. Did the miscue change the meaning of the text?
2. What does the miscue reveal about the reader's knowledge and use of words?
3. What was the reader thinking at the time the miscue was read?
4. What are some context clues the reader used or might have used?
5. What kinds of connections can you make to what you read?

Keep in mind that teachers and students may adjust the list by adding a question that reflects another strategy being studied in guided reading groups or whole-class instruction. Common strategies might be the use of inference and/or summary to guide comprehension.

THE IMPORTANCE OF RETELLING DURING RMA

The second part of any RMA session is a discussion of the student's retelling (also tape recorded). It is our experience from working with a wide range of reading abilities that one of the most powerful tools in building comprehension is a simple retelling or summarizing of what was read. The teacher asks the child to "retell" the story in the reader's own words. During this part of the RMA session, the group listens to the taped retelling after discussing miscues, adds to the retelling, or focuses on reading between the lines or beyond. It is important to continue to emphasize that meaning is at the heart of reading if readers are to consider their miscues valid attempts to understand the text.

Children are encouraged to discuss the meaning and thinking behind their retellings just as they explore the nuances and meanings of language in their miscues. For example, instead of merely discussing a character's actions, a question may come up about the character's vulnerability, his or her ethical stance, or how his or her actions impacted the lives of others. Another question for discussion may include how the character speaks or acts based on culture or community. Careful attention to student reading interests and maintaining a broad scope of genres in children's literature is integral to supporting authenticity and critical inquiry during these reading discussions.

RMA sessions coupled with carefully chosen literature from content provide strong support for content reading thus extending opportunities for integrated curriculum. For example, a segment of text about the Montgomery bus strikes or the adaptations of spiders provide another avenue for discussion during retellings about content being covered within the curriculum. Providing support for content-area reading in ways students may have not experienced before assists students' knowledge about the importance of reading comprehension across the curriculum. Depending on the effectiveness of previous teachers, some students believe that reading strategies only apply to reading narrative text or the text they encounter in guided reading groups. RMA is a critical tool for students struggling to read many types of text, including textbooks and other nonfiction text. Comprehension strategies often provide the focus for RMA conversations.

BEFORE GROUPING FOR RMA

Prior to grouping for RMA, the teacher demonstrates to the entire class the RMA process and gives them multiple examples of miscues to discuss prior to the RMA small-group sessions. When about 90% of the class seems confident with the process, the teacher proceeds to the formation of RMA groups. We learned that some readers will "catch on" more quickly in the small group format so there's no need to prolong the process; just be sure you check for understanding once the groups are formed. Understanding the small-group process (roles and responsibilities of the members) is critical to student comfort level during the RMA conversations. The questions for RMA discussion are posted where RMA group members can easily see them in order to refer to them during discussion. This really helps keep the conversation from lagging, which can occur when initiating RMA (not an issue once the process is underway).

Keeping Track of the Data Over Time

Probably the most challenging aspects of implementing RMA are collecting, organizing, and storing the data. In this chapter and previously, we suggest procedures for teachers that we have found helpful, but we also encourage teachers to develop procedures that work best for their classrooms. The important thing to remember is to have a system for collection and storage so that the data is easily retrieved, analyzed, and shared with students as well as parents, resource teachers, or administrators. When the teacher has listened to the recorded readings from each student in a group and marked the miscues, the miscues are then transferred to the Simplified Miscue Organizer (found in Resource G), and then the teacher puts the organizer back into the student's folder. She or he may also use the Retelling Guide found in Resources C and D (one is for fiction, one for nonfiction or expository text).

As mentioned in Chapter 4, Vicki collected the data from miscue taping literacy stations in a large three-ring binder behind the first tab. Data organized for the actual RMA sessions was kept in the next tab in the same notebook and contained all of the forms Vicki used during RMA processes. It included the miscue retelling guides, inventory sheets, and interview forms. She kept several copies of each so they were always at hand when needed.

Following these initial tabs was a tab for each student in the classroom labeled with their first name. First, behind the tab is each student's beginning-of-the-year completed reading inventory. Next, the original, marked miscue recording sheets were filed from first to next to next, chronologically, with the transcribed retellings. Behind each of these were the miscue retelling guides Vicki completed for each student. The RMA notebook Vicki constructed was kept with all other teaching materials she used on a daily basis. As we mentioned earlier, other teachers may wish to have separate file folders for each student.

Student Folders

Student folders contained copies of the students' marked miscue recording sheets. These were in chronological order so that it was easy to pull another RMA session's sheet out to sometimes compare miscues. The folders also contained miscue-recording sheets from other students and an audiotape for each student. These folders were color-coded by group and marked with individual student names.

They were kept upright in a plastic bin so that audiotapes were not lost, and students could see at a glance where their folders were stored. The folders in plastic bins were kept near the workstation for ease when students were audiotaping.

Choice of Reading Text

Typescripts of about 150 to 250 words may come from any reading text, but the choice of text may also provide the teacher more control over the purpose and learning outcome of the RMA conversation. For example, the use of nonfiction text is recommended for use during RMA preparatory sessions to facilitate increased understanding of text that students struggle with that they might not self-select and that help to build skills in content-area reading. In the RMA conversation, all of the group members then benefit from a discussion of strategies to understand nonfiction text, thus immersing students in content area curriculum often lacking in traditional guided reading or basal reading instruction.

Handing Out the Student Folders

First assign each group of students a folder color—different for each group. The folders should contain an audiocassette tape and the first reading passage for the groups, each enlarged with lines numbered for easy reference after coding. Accordion folders work the best—preferably plastic with fasteners. Next, show the students how to work the tape recorder and tell them your expectations. For example, Vicki demonstrated operation of the tape recorder, noting that she would be present for each student's first reading and retelling but expected them to be able to operate the tape recorder alone after the first session. Later, she listened to the taped readings and retellings and marked them according to standard miscue procedures explained in Chapter 4. The marked typescript was then placed back into the student's folder. Procedures for marking the miscues are discussed in Chapter 4 along with simple marking guides. Teachers who have conducted Running Records (Clay, 2000; Johnston, 1997) will find the organizational processes similar, but the analysis of miscues is somewhat different. In addition, retellings are not always included in the running record process.

Beginning the RMA Conversations

For the sake of building understanding of how the RMA conversations work, we advise that RMA sessions be held at least once a week during the start up use of the strategy. RMA conversations are held about one to two months prior to introducing Socratic Circles. They may be held prior to guided reading discussions, incorporated into guided reading as part of the "after reading" discussion, or prior to computer-generated comprehension tests or other reading instruction that the teacher may be required to use by the school district as a way of orienting the reader toward greater comprehension, vocabulary awareness, and confidence in the reading process with an emphasis on building on reader strengths.

Laying the Ground Rules

Students need guidance and support if the RMA conversation is to be successful. Establishing ground rules for discussion and behavior is critical to the success of the process. You may have already set up classroom rules or guidelines for discussion groups. Draw on those as a framework, remind students to use the "miscue" terminology using the posters on display for help, and provide them with the following questions to focus their discussion:

- Did the miscue change the meaning of the text?
- What does the miscue tell us about what the reader knows about language?
- What was the reader thinking at the time the miscue was read?
- What kinds of connections was the reader making?
- What prior knowledge does the reader have that might have helped understand the text? (This question came from part of the state reading curriculum standards and was a concept Vicki reminded students of across the curriculum.)
- Was the miscue a "smart" or an "okay" miscue?

When one group's folders are ready, revisit the ground rules and post questions with the students, then begin the RMA conversation. It is best to begin one group at a time.

We think it is important to mention that many teachers may harbor doubts about young students' readiness for RMA group discussions; Vicki was one of those teachers. What Vicki later realized from watching the videotapes of some of the RMA sessions was that the process of RMA actually taught listening skills far more than any advanced preparation she could give them. She regretted not starting the process much sooner and using RMA conversations to enrich and extend some of the more traditional venues such as guided reading. Vicki and Rita both believe that setting high expectations for all learners is critical to achieving their learning potential.

BUT WILL THEY GET IT?

Teachers sometimes question whether children are developmentally "ready" for retrospectively analyzing and discussing miscues and retellings and whether they grasp the nomenclature needed to explain the cognitive processes associated with reading. The answer is a resounding yes! Readers as young as Vicki's third graders quickly learn the terminology associated with RMA as well as the kinds of questions that help them better understand the reading process and themselves as readers.

It is surprising to teachers how seriously readers shoulder their roles during RMA. Students in Vicki's class clearly had high expectations for themselves and peers during RMA sessions and willingly accepted responsibility for group participation without being reminded or prompted. Modeling by other students facilitates the functioning of the group more than waiting to get started based on each student's complete understanding of the process. As is often the case in learning, the understanding comes with, rather than before, the interactive experience.

RMA conversations provide teachers with a practical but highly effective approach to improving students' reading as well as their understanding that reading is a process, not a single subject to be learned and that all readers bring some strengths to the act of reading. Using RMA procedures, students and teachers explore reading as a meaning-making process by questioning, examining, and making decisions about reading miscues and their retelling of text. These procedures may be utilized in reading workshop, guided reading, Accelerated Reader procedures, and literature discussion groups. Rotation of groups is (and should be) a part of RMA.

REFLECTION

The use of RMA with younger children in a whole-class setting is indeed powerful. That primary age children can address complex questions gives teachers, administrators, literacy coaches, and parents a whole new perspective on how to approach the teaching of reading and a surprisingly deep understanding of how language works. Although some preparation of the students ahead of time is necessary, the time spent in laying the groundwork is critical. Figuring out the process comes with practice for students and teachers, but establishing purpose, rationale, and definitions initially ensures the success of the reading discussions. How these critical thinking strategies carry over into other aspects of the classroom curriculum will be discussed in subsequent chapters.

Since no miscue is without meaning, and all readers miscue, RMA is a process of "revaluing" the reader (Goodman, 1996a, p. 15). Teachers using RMA recognize existing as well as potential reading strengths, thus helping learners identify reading strategies that will prove more effective than those they may currently use. In other words, instead of counting errors, the rationale behind the miscues is explored and made explicit to the reader during RMA conversations.

During RMA, the readers' responses to the meaning behind the miscues of pronunciation and retelling are also valuable because they empower the reader to own the reading process and to learn what it means to be a proficient reader. In addition, RMA provides an opportunity for group members to take on the role of peer mentors, thus releasing the responsibility (Pearson and Gallagher, 1983) for teaching to the children and, as the transcripts in this book demonstrate, the children quickly take on that responsibility with seriousness and respect.

6 Assessing Reading Performance Through RMA

"In" for "into" is a smart miscue.
The other one is an okay miscue.

—Nellie, a third grader

This chapter will do the following:

- Briefly discuss how reading assessment is characterized in Retrospective Miscue Analysis (RMA) and in Socratic Circles
- Present an overview of the learning needs in Vicki's classroom
- Discuss the ways readers may be viewed through formal assessments
- Provide some pre- and post-assessment measures that assist with the implementation of the RMA process
- Discuss how the classroom community acclimates to the language of RMA

ASSESSMENT CHARACTERIZED IN RMA AND IN SOCRATIC CIRCLES

It is important to remember that assessment is not defined in this book as a summative evaluation. It is a formative, ongoing process that continually informs instruction, values the reader's strengths (Strickland & Strickland, 2000), and encourages student voice. Nellie's comment above is an example of a student's assessment of the miscue.

RMA is largely characterized by teacher observations, documented by some sort of anecdotal record keeping during the RMA conversations. It is also characterized by the patterns of reading behaviors and strategies used by the readers and the patterns of response the readers of each RMA group show during the RMA conversations. For example, what are the readers focusing on—fluency, meaning, the nuances of language, vocabulary, and so on, and what triggers those responses?

Substantial information about patterns of reading emerges as the teacher analyzes the miscues, but when students analyze their own miscues, the teacher not only is privy to hearing the rationale behind the miscue but why choosing a particular miscue for analysis was important. The reader's developing proficiency in comprehension and the emergent behaviors or responses that signal changing perceptions of self as reader foster a wealth of assessment information. Keeping track of the data is easy when the teacher looks at patterns from each RMA group then compares those data patterns across groups, deciding what strengths are common and what areas need developing, either as a class, as a group, or as individuals. This response to readers and the reading process is an authentic and powerful approach to organizing for differentiated instruction in reading and across the curriculum. For example, each of Vicki's RMA groups discussed miscues of hyphenation. Their interpretations and questions led to many mini-lessons from which the entire class benefited and examples for classroom discussion came directly from their experiences in RMA conversations.

The current focus in schools is upon using experimental data (studies that investigate causation) to drive instruction; therefore, these can inadvertently lead teachers to look at weaknesses in students' abilities and skills. The focus of RMA begins by looking at the readers' strengths.

VICKI'S CLASSROOM

We will begin with a brief overview of Vicki's third grade classroom so teachers might see how RMA may be implemented in a challenging setting. Fifteen third graders entered Vicki's classroom in the fall. Four students were on medication for attention difficulties; in addition, one student received medication for depression. Three students were on individualized education plans (IEPs) for learning disabilities or language processing difficulties, and one student was on an IEP for speech articulation. Two students struggled with anxiety difficulties. Students' families during the year were impacted by a stepfather's suicide attempts, a father's terminal illness, divorce, and unemployment. The class was small in number;

therefore, they were assigned to what was called the "little classroom," a remodeled teacher's workroom.

VIEWING STUDENTS THROUGH FORMAL ASSESSMENTS

In addition to the overall variation of learning needs, there was also a wide range of reading abilities assessed through standard measures. Due to a district mandate, Vicki was also piloting a new phonemic awareness, phonics, symbol, and visual imagery program in which the students were administered summative reading assessments during the first two weeks of school. The range of scores for all students on the assessments were as follows:

Name of Test	*Range of Scores*
Lindamood Test of Auditory Conceptualization (LAC) (a test of phonemic awareness)	PreK to 4.2
Woodcock Reading Mastery Test (WRMT)	
Word Attack Subtest (a test of decoding)	1.8 to 7
Wide Range Achievement Test (WRAT)	
Spelling Subtest (a test of spelling ability)	2.8 to 5
Slosson Oral Reading Test (SORT) (a test of sight words)	2.7 to 6.7
Gray Oral Reading Test (GORT) (Paragraph Reading Subtest)	
Reading Rate	<1.0 to 5.4
Reading Accuracy	<1.0 to 3.2
Reading Fluency	<1.0 to 4.0
Reading Comprehension	<1.0 to 6.7

The range of reading abilities was challenging. Vicki's rationale for choosing RMA to develop reading instruction was that it was flexible enough to continue to assess and improve the various reading levels and distinctive learning scenarios presented by her students, thus providing them opportunities for the authentic assessment of their own reading processes that went beyond standardized, summative measures.

PRE- AND POST-ASSESSMENT: MEASURES THAT HELP TEACHERS ORGANIZE FOR RMA

Before initiating RMA conversations and Socratic Circles, it is a good idea to select some sort of easy pre- and post-informal assessment of student comprehension levels (*frustration*, *instructional*, or *independent* are categorizations often associated with informal reading inventories), or if you are using the STAR test associated with the Reading Renaissance's Accelerated Reader Program (for more information, see http://www.renlearn.com/sr/), those levels will be readily available. These assessments may be simple comprehension interviews or quizzes administered individually at the child's instructional level of reading, or they may be levels already established through a standardized test or an informal reading inventory. The Qualitative Reading Inventory (Leslie, & Caldwell, 1988) is an example of an informal reading inventory, and while there are many others, most follow a similar format.

The use of informal reading inventories are found as a part of many published textbook programs or may be used independently by teachers or literacy specialists. For the informal reading inventory, students are asked to read a short piece of text and retell or answer comprehension questions over the reading. Vocabulary proficiency and oral reading levels are calculated based on the controlled vocabulary of the reading selections and assist the teacher in forming flexible reading groups in which the make up of the group may change as the abilities or needs of the readers change. Informal reading inventories provide quick and easy methods of pre- and post-assessment while the RMA process, itself, is a continuous informal reading assessment involving students and teachers. Typically, informal reading inventories provide the teacher with baseline data of student reading levels—independent, instructional, or frustration levels—although experienced teachers may feel confident in creating flexible ability groups based on their observations and work with the student. Using both or a combination of informal reading inventories, patterns of reading behaviors during RMA, and standardized tests presents varied qualitative and quantitative documentation of reading progress and proficiency over time.

Sharing the Knowledge

Critical to the effective use of classroom assessment is the involvement of the students in the assessment and instructional process. For example, if you hold reading conferences periodically with students, ask for their feedback on what they are learning from the RMA groups and eventually share pre- and post-assessment results from other data with them. Integrate the strategies associated with RMA into your teaching routine so you are not only assessing learning but also the effectiveness of the strategies you have selected on student perceptions of learning. Simple questions such as, *"What's working for you in RMA and what is not?"* suffice to offer insightful information that allows the teacher and the student to monitor individual reading development as well as the development of the RMA groups overall.

Assessing Reading and Perceptions of Reading

It is helpful to keep in mind that while classroom (informal) or standardized (formal) reading assessments may reveal useful information about the students' reading ability, they may be missing or provide virtually no data about how the students view or perceive themselves as readers, which is critical to becoming a successful, confident reader. The assessments may not show the students' definition of reading, the strategies they use as readers, or how they feel about reading—all factors that guide reading curriculum and instruction; therefore, we highly recommend that teachers document student perceptions of reading. The reader must also know that reading is supposed to make sense; if the text does not make sense to them, then they are not reading. Building this awareness is often most effectively accomplished through the use of reading perceptions measures.

One instrument to use for documenting student perceptions of reading is the Burke Reading Interview or some adaptation thereof. The Burke essentially documents how the student views the reading process asking such questions as, "Who is a good reader you know?" "What makes a good reader?" or "When you come to a word you don't know, what do you do?" The questions often clearly reveal how the student views himself or herself as a reader and strategies used to read. Before giving the miscue analysis, many teachers use the Burke Reading Interview (Burke, 1987) to identify students' perceived reading behaviors and attitudes. An example of the Burke Reading Interview is located in Resource H.

Using the Burke Interview as an initial evaluation tool helps teachers to better know and value readers. They can then compare the readers' perceptions of their reading behaviors with strategies actually used during the reading. Moore and Gilles (2005) further explain,

> Some readers say what they think the teacher wants to hear, while others are quite honest. Many young readers have not thought about what they do as readers; they are less metacognitive. For these readers, the Burke Interview answers are more a reflection of what they have been taught [rather than actual practice]. (p.16)

Vicki found the Burke Interview too daunting to administer to an entire class of third-grade students in the first quarter of the year. Previous experiences with fourth- and fifth-grade readers led her to prefer asking students to take their time and respond in writing to the Burke Interview questions so that she had their answers in writing; they could keep them in their reading portfolios and refer to them, making modifications as they wanted, and discuss them during reading conferences with her or with Vicki and their parents. This particular group of third graders was generally not used to writing much yet, and the length of the Burke seemed overwhelming to most of them, so she decided on another approach. This included documenting student perceptions of reading using the following three-question survey conducted with each reader at the beginning of the year.

- What is reading?
- How do you read?
- What do you do to read?

The students' answers to the questions were brief, but they clearly revealed the factors the children associated with reading. For example, Autumn, one of the third graders, responded to the first question with, "It's where you take a book and open it. Then there will be words. You take it home to your mom and dad and when they read. You try." Figure 6.1 shows Michael's (another third grader) response to the initial survey.

The children were candid and cooperative with their responses. See Resource I for a reproducible copy of the survey. Vicki's survey is designed to be a quick and efficient approach to use with younger readers; however, it can be modified to use with older or more advanced readers as well. In addition, teachers may want to add questions to the survey as the reading abilities of the children evolve or other questions about reading interests or habits surface.

Vicki actually prefers using the Burke Reading Interview or a reflection tool called "Reflecting on Reading" from *Still Learning to Read* (Sibberson & Szymusiak, 2003). However, she realized soon after the beginning of the year that the third-grade students would have difficulty completing a written reading inventory without a great deal of support. She was invested in learning exactly what the students were thinking and interested in their authentic responses. Consider Autumn's response to asking what she likes to read on the "Reflecting on Reading" tool (Sibberson & Szymusiak, 2003): "Magazines, school books, chances to win stuff on the back of boxes." A response such as this is not possible until students understand that reading is everywhere, a concept Vicki promotes and reinforces in her classroom. Another student's response to the Sibberson

Figure 6.1 Michael's Survey Responses

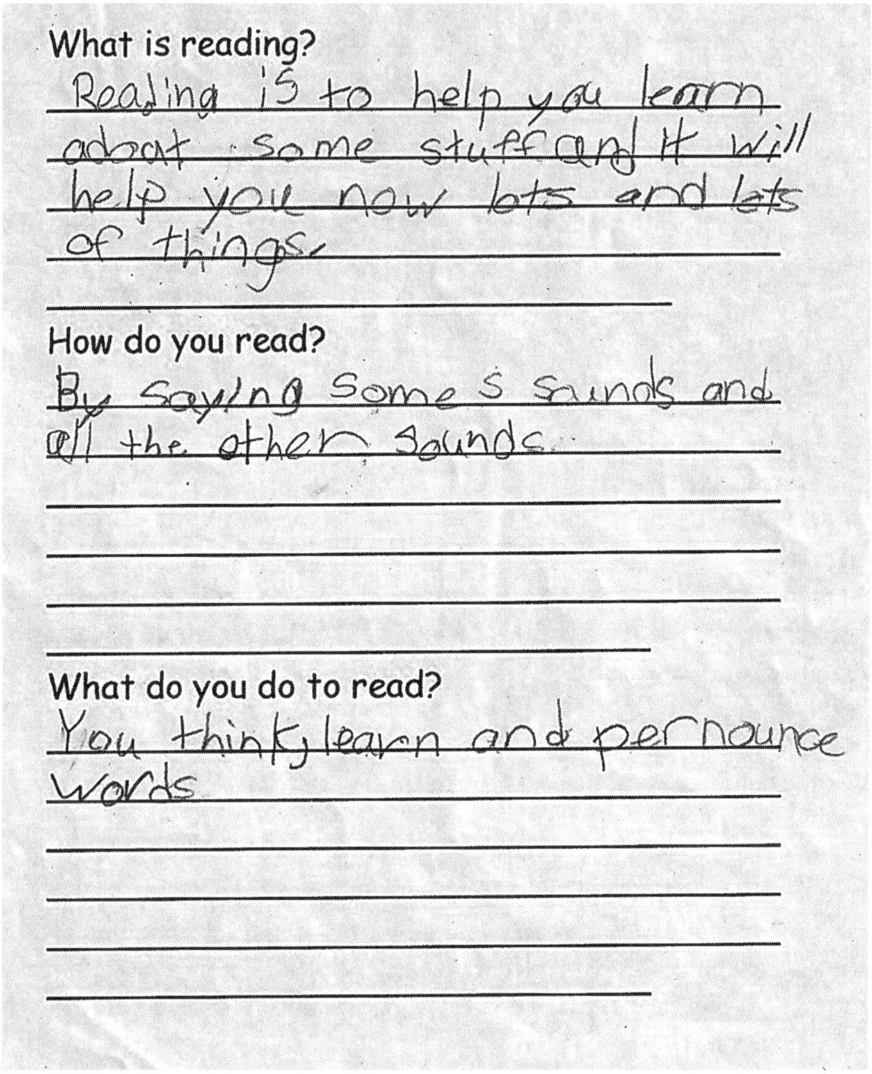

What is reading?

Reading is to help you learn adout some stuff and it will help you now lots and lots of things.

How do you read?

By saying some s sounds and all the other sounds.

What do you do to read?

You think, learn and pernounce words

and Szymusiak (2003) survey "Reflecting on Reading" comes from Jaimie and appears in Figure 6.2.

When teaching fifth grade, Vicki used two informal inventories to establish a reading baseline for her students. The first was an interest inventory completed the first full day of school that asked what students had read over the summer, what reading goals they wanted to set for themselves during the year, and what genres they were interested in reading during the year. (All names of the fifth-grade children are pseudonyms.) One student, Rene, wrote the titles of the books she had read over

Figure 6.2 Jaimie's Reflections on Reading

Reflecting on Reading

Name Jaimie Date 3/10/05

How would you describe yourself as a reader?
a good reader a person who under-stands most books

What are you currently reading?
I am reading a book called The Boxcar Children

What kinds of things do you like to read?
I Like to read Nonfiction and fiction chapter books

What kinds of things do you not like to read?
I do not like facule books they are notesea to read

What are you going to read next?
I am going to read Anna on the farm next

How do you choose the books you read?
Mrs. Seeger helps me pick my books I know the books I should pick

What do you do when you get stuck?
I would try to sound the word out and if I can not get it

What do you do when you start to read each day?
I reread a paragraf that I read yesterday.

How do you keep track of the characters in the books you are reading?
I do not realy kep track of the caripter

What kind of reading is easy for you?
fiction Chapter books

What kind of reading is hard for you?
Nonfiction Books (chapterbooks)

SOURCE: From *Still Learning to Read: Teaching Students in Grades 3–6* by Franki Sibberson and Karen Szymusiak, © 2003, with permission of Stenhouse Publishers (www.stenhouse.com).

the summer and noted, "I think I am reading great historical fiction books because it tells you a lot about back then." Thomas wrote, "I notice most books I read are nonfiction. I would genrally [sic] like to read books about war history and wild life books [sic]." And Taylor set this goal for himself, "What I have learned was that I like thick books fiction and adventer [sic] the most. This year I am going to read like crazy."

Later in the year, Vicki administered a slightly modified Burke Reading Interview to four students participating in the RMA process who she felt would benefit from articulating how they perceived themselves as readers. As a result, she received valuable information honoring the reader's perception of themselves as readers. For example, Rene has a clear picture of herself as a reader and the biggest obstacle she faces when she states on the Burke, "Because I never remember what happens and I don't do good on the test (Accelerated Reader tests)." Suzanne knows she is a good reader when she reads about animals. She writes, "Because I am in to [sic] animal books and I read them alot easyer [sic]." Katie realized her limitations for reading aloud but also set a goal for herself related to reading aloud when she said, "I would like to read out loud better than I do now. When I read aloud I get nervese [sic] and I don't read as good."

Recently Vicki administered the Burke Reading Interview to Troy (pseudonym), a student she tutored over the summer months. Troy requested the tutoring convinced that tutoring from last summer helped him achieve good grades during this past year. He has little sense that he really knows quite a bit about himself as a reader; he also has a good grasp of what he still needs to work on when he reads. When asked about someone he considers a good reader, Troy cited a peer in his class from the past year. This seventh-grade male equates being a good reader with being a good speller and getting the words right when he says, "He doesn't slur his words." He also noted the "good" reader reads at a good tempo. When she asked Troy if he was a good reader he stated, "Yeah, I'm okay. I don't slur words. I'm not choppy. I stop at periods and commas for breath." When asked what he would like to do better as a reader, he said, "Read faster. I would like to know all the words I don't know."

As a seventh grader, Troy knows quite a bit about reading fluency but is convinced he needs someone else to help him when he cites parents, teachers, friends, and "even your brother" to help you when struggling with reading. Vicki's goal in tutoring Troy was to boost his knowledge of independent reading strategies by engaging him in a miscue analysis process showing him what he is already doing well and what else he might consider doing to read successfully and believe in himself as a competent reader. Figure 6.3 is a completed Burke Interview Vicki conducted with Troy's responses.

Documenting Learning Gains and Continuous Evaluation of the Learners

The RMA folders provide individualized assessment documentation of each reader in the classroom and are easily maintained by the teacher

Figure 6.3 Burke Interview With Troy

Burke Reading Interview

Name Troy (pseudonym) Age 13 Date 6/30/08

Occupation Student Education Level entering 7th grade

Sex Male Interview Setting home

1. When you are reading and come to something you don't know, what do you do?
   I pause. If it's a word, I try to sound it out. If I didn't know the word, I would ask someone. If they didn't know, I'd ask the teacher. If I'm at home, I would sound it out, look on the computer, ask my parents if they are at home.

   Do you ever do anything else?
   No.

2. Who is a good reader you know?
   Trevor (pseudonym). [Trevor is a classmate also entering the 7th grade.]

3. What makes Trevor a good reader?
   He uses or acts like he is a character in the book. He can spell real well. He doesn't slur words. He reads at a good tempo.

4. Do you think Trevor ever comes to something she/he doesn't know?

   __X__ Yes _____ No

5. (Yes) When Trevor comes to something she/he doesn't know, what do you think he/she does?
   He asks parents, teachers, or a friend.

   (No) Suppose __Trevor__ comes to something she/he doesn't know. What do you think she/he would do?

6. If you knew someone was having trouble reading, how would you help that person?
   Tell them, "If you are struggling reading, ask your parents to read with you, or a reading buddy, a teacher, sometimes even your brother."

7. What would a/your teacher do to help that person?
   Probably suggest summer school, a tutor, or take free time to go back there and help read with him.

8. How did you learn to read?
   Just a natural habit. From Kindergarten. From learning how to spell. Parents helping me.

(Continued)

Figure 6.3 (Continued)

9. What would you like to do better as a reader?
   Read faster. I would like to know all the words I don't know.

10. Do you think you are a good reader? Why?
    Yea, I'm okay. I don't slur words. I'm not choppy. I stop at periods and commas for breath. I like challenges. I like big books. [Troy is currently reading The Inventions of Hugo Cabret, *a novel that includes text and graphics, by Brian Selznick. It is 550 pages in length, and Troy is impressed with how "thick" the book is and how engaged he is with reading it.]*

and the student. They are individualized because the texts you ask the children to read are slightly challenging (written at an instructional level) to each reader, address their interests or needs, and the miscues you select for discussion on the Simplified Miscue Organizer (Resource G) are carefully chosen for RMA group discussion and analysis. These folders may be shared with parents and other teachers to suggest patterns of reading behaviors observed during RMA and beyond.

To use RMA outcomes to inform instruction, the teacher periodically looks through the Simplified Miscue Organizers, keeping a tally of the kinds of reading miscues the readers are making—always looking for patterns of reader response. Then, during guided reading or the RMA sessions, one may suggest strategies for strengthening reading development such as the Think Aloud mentioned previously in Chapter 5 with continued discussion in Chapter 8. Alternatively, Donna Ogle suggests involving the readers in the ongoing assessment and documentation process by asking them to create their own group progress charts much like you would construct a *KWL* chart (*what I know, what I want to know,* and *what I've learned*) (Vacca & Vacca, 2007). In this case, the KWL would focus on miscues and retellings. And perhaps the KWL could be expanded to include a third column—*What do I want to improve upon in my reading*? The group should be asked to provide specific examples under each category based on the reader or readers' miscues. This process provides ownership and power to the readers and helps the teacher with the assessment process!

ACCLIMATING THE CLASSROOM TO THE LANGUAGE OF RMA

Earlier in the book, we suggest using the Burke Reading Interview or others to explore how students define reading and the kind of reader they perceive themselves to be. This kind of exploration introduces the inquiring climate of the RMA process, which is immediately student-centered rather than formal test-score focused. (We suggest teachers administer the Burke to each other or to a child for practice and comparison of answers. You might be surprised!)

Once this climate is set, the language of RMA becomes the venue for readers of all abilities to discuss perceptions of themselves as readers through the miscues they and other group members make. As mentioned earlier, prior to beginning RMA with the students, Vicki surveyed the third graders about their conceptions of reading. The results of those surveys provided insight into how the students viewed themselves as readers before beginning RMA processes—a valuable piece of information for teachers assembling working RMA groups and valuable information to share with the readers.

When readers began to examine their miscues and retellings, they were encouraged to think about their perceptions of themselves as readers and to better understand that a substitution, omission, insertion, or any of the other miscue identifiers were actually strategies they used to problem solve the text and that they used these strategies in an attempt to make meaning. Not always were they successful, of course, but understanding the reading process gave them greater control and empowered them as readers as they discussed the miscues and decided if the strategies they were using were working or not.

Vicki always encouraged the RMA participants to point out the reader's strengths, and soon, that became second nature to them as they problem solved the meaning behind the miscue. Knowing that there is always a reason for the miscue takes away the notion of right or wrong response, replacing it with something much like scientific inquiry and the children, much like Vicki's fourth and fifth graders in previous years, thrived in that atmosphere of empowered learning. They became young linguists who discovered they knew a lot about language and reading.

Take a look at the quotation at the beginning of this chapter by Nellie during an RMA session. She is very adept at deciding when miscues affect the meaning of text and when the miscue has caused a problem for the reader. When there are opportunities to point out "smart" miscues, the teacher needs to seize the moment being careful not to leave the impression that all miscues are high level. This detracts from opportunities to discuss the reading process and language systems behind the miscues and leaves the RMA group with little to discuss. The questions that always help readers focus are *Does the miscue make sense?* and *Does the miscue sound like language?*

Later, after many opportunities to explore the reading process through their miscues, individual behaviors within the RMA groups demonstrate changed views of themselves as readers and the reasons for reading. The survey entitled "Reflecting on Reading" (Sibberson & Szymusiak, 2003) introduced in this chapter provides useful information about how diverse classroom communities view themselves as readers. These views are later expressed within RMA groups and the Socratic Circle sessions using the language of miscue coding to express observations of the reading process.

REFLECTION

Sometimes we tend to "see" our students through test scores rather than "knowing" our students as readers. The quotation from Conrad at the beginning of Chapter 3 suggests that tests might not capture a complete picture of the reader's comprehension. When that happens, students also develop those perceptions. Remember the student Dorothy Watson worked with who insisted he couldn't read and that she should check his test scores to prove it?

When asked about a student's reading success or lack of it, we may talk about the number of books they have read, the range of books they would be comfortable reading, or their percentage correct on tests. The work within RMA gives us insight into how readers "think" and process text as they read. It is like no other process we, as teachers, have engaged in previously.

Because students are articulating what happens when they read, we see them in a whole new light—a critical piece often missing from our view of students as readers. For many, our view of students has been clouded by assessment that focused on specific skills but failed to see the child as a reader. Like the reader we mentioned in the introduction to the book who insisted he couldn't read and that his test scores proved it, a cycle of perceived failure often begins. This notion of failure may be linked to the entity theory of learning (Dweck & Bempechet, 1983) wherein children or young adolescents concede that the ability to learn is innate. After so many failed attempts to read documented by test scores or other labels, they may well believe they are incapable of becoming good readers.

Documenting student learning using multiple assessment strategies gives the teacher a much more in-depth understanding of each reader's knowledge and skills, which led to more informed instructional decisions. In addition to assessments that assist the classroom teacher in pinpointing instructional and independent reading levels, the use of interviews and surveys to find out about students' interests, self-views as a reader, and what they already know about their strengths and weaknesses contribute to a holistic view of the students as readers. The miscue organizers and documented discussions provide insightful data—data that speak volumes beyond numbers, percentages, percentiles, and lexiles. Instead, a teacher gains a view of a student individually rather than as part of a collective group.

7 Informing Instruction Through RMA

I felt like I really understood this piece.

—Jennie, a third grader

This chapter will do the following:

- Explore how the (Retrospective Miscue Analysis) RMA process guides instruction
- Provide suggestions for documenting RMA learning gains and needs of the individuals, the groups, and the classroom as a whole
- Discuss how patterns of miscues can be easily used to further guide reading instruction with the use of simple classroom research techniques

THE RMA PROCESS GUIDES INSTRUCTION: SPECIFIC EXAMPLES

Two Introductory Vignettes

Elizabeth, a reader struggling to comprehend any text she read independently but functioning at a high level in guided reading groups, made up words for those she did not know when she encountered them in the text. During RMA, Vicki discovered Elizabeth's misread words and understood immediately why she was having so much difficulty with independently read text and with textbook reading in content areas. In guided reading (Fountas & Pinnell, 1996), an instructional strategy that matches ability level with reading materials, the text Elizabeth was reading was leveled so carefully (most published materials target the instructional level or the level at which the reader is able to read the text silently or orally with about 80% accuracy in word recognition and comprehension) she did not have as many opportunities to try to read and decode words she did not know. In subsequent RMA conversations, her peers commented on her misread words and, through thoughtful analyzing and reflection, helped her realize what she was doing. Later in this chapter, a detailed vignette is given that shows Elizabeth's miscues and Vicki's thought processes as she analyzed Elizabeth's reading.

During another session with this same RMA group, the discussion is focused on Jennie's tape recording and miscues related to words she is unfamiliar with in reading, but has heard in conversation. The group is giving Jennie advice on what to do when she encounters words she is unable to read successfully. Their discussion assists Vicki in seeing the word solving strategies students are using.

Vicki: Let's pretend for a moment that you're reading independently. What could you do to figure out those words?

Jennie: I could stop, look at it, and think of a couple of words that I've heard before.

Phoenix: Connect it?

Elizabeth: Look it up.

Jennie: Kind of chunk up that word.

Phoenix: Connect the word in the assignment to words you know what they mean.

Vicki: I think all the ideas that you all have mentioned are good strategies to fix things when you run into words that you don't know. And I think when we're reading, we have to constantly ask ourselves, "Is that language I can understand?" And if not, *maybe* ask somebody, but I would prefer that you look at words around it.

Ron: I ask my mom if I don't understand.

Phoenix: You can also take out words in the bigger word and if you know what they mean, you can kind of get a better idea. It might not be exact, but it will give you a better idea.

Vicki learned a great deal about her own teaching because of the audiotaping and videotaping that occurred for RMA. During one discussion about miscues with the striving readers, she missed an opportunity to follow up on a connection made by Molly. She realized it only after viewing the videotaping of the session. In retrospect, she regrets not elaborating on Molly's connection, as striving readers particularly need reinforcement of their efforts to make connections to the texts they are reading independently. However, she was able to use the information she gained from looking at the videotaped session to follow up on Molly's connection and to make certain Molly knew that her miscues may be occurring because of her mental connections to some other text she has read.

Jackson: On line 407, he said *shoots* not *shots*.

Vicki: We had a lot of miscues on that word. Why do you think we did?

Abigail: They look alike . . . .

Vicki: Can you think of another word from another book that you've been reading that might have affected your reading of *shots*?

Molly: *The Box Car Children*

DOCUMENTING THE RMA CONVERSATIONS

By the end of the school year, Vicki had many forms of documentation for the RMA sessions for each group of students, including transcribed miscues onto text passages, retelling recording sheets, audiotapes for each student, and videotapes of all sessions. The transcribed miscues provide helpful documentation of the kinds of miscues each student makes, but more importantly, provide the kind of documentation needed to make informed decisions about instruction in reading. The teacher should informally and formally analyze these, looking for patterns, corrective behaviors, and reduction in miscues throughout the sessions. Having multiple measures of student learning portrays a much broader picture of student reading development than any single measure such as a standardized test.

The reproducible retelling recording sheets (Resources C and D) are especially useful for realizing that students' comprehension of text may focus primarily on details and reveal when readers are unable to summarize text meaningfully and efficiently. This data informs instruction. For example, analysis of these sheets enabled Vicki to work on very specific reading comprehension strategies during other guided reading sessions. An example of a retelling from expository text from Kathie appears in Figure 7.1.

Figure 7.1 Kathie's Retelling Responses to Expository Text

Retelling Guide for Expository Text

Name: Date: 3/1/05

Name of Text: Rosa Parks

Directions: Score each of the following unaided retelling responses on a scale of 0–10 depending on the clarity and depth of the response. Teachers may wish to have the answers prepared ahead of time to facilitate scoring. These may be stored in the reader's portfolio or with assessment records for RMA or CRMA.

Score	Item	Aided	Unaided
1	All important facts were recalled.	___	↓
1	Supporting ideas were recalled.	___	↓
0	Ideas were recalled in logical order.	___	↓
7	Reader recalled important conclusions.	___	↓
3	Reader stated valid inferences.	___	↓

Comments: This piece is about Rosa Parks. If it wasn't for Rosa Parks, we would still be segregated. This story was about a black girl. She's one of my American heroes.

SOURCE: Adapted from Moore & Gilles, 2005, with permission.

Using videotapes to assess instruction allows the teacher to be two places at once. And videotapes provide unique documentation of learning, permitting the teacher to see group dynamics at work and the ability and/or inability of individual students to contribute in a meaningful way. For example, while Vicki worked diligently to let students lead the RMA conversations, if she noted behavior patterns from the videotapes that were hampering a student's ability to perform in the group, she worked at carefully redirecting that behavior during the next RMA session. It was also through the videotapes that Vicki saw how animated her students were when engaged in such an important, meaningful, and compelling process: heads were cocked to the side as they considered a possible explanation, hands demonstrated length of sentences or moved up and down to mimic expression, and eyebrows furrowed when words were puzzling. She listened to students working through confusion and easily identified the moment when their critical discussions about their reading miscues or retellings provided clarity for them.

FINDING PATTERNS OF READING MISCUES

It is not unusual for classroom teachers to employ action research strategies for organizing patterns of learning they are observing in the classroom (Moore & Gilles, 2005). To better identify patterns of reading response that allow more informed instructional decisions in teaching, it is useful to conduct simple tallies. For example, Vicki looked for recurring patterns in the children's oral reading and in their retellings and kept track of these by coding the common miscues with a yellow highlighter and sorting other kinds of miscues using various other colors: green for substitutions, blue for reversals, and so on.

Elizabeth's behavior underscores the importance of looking for these patterns. As noted earlier, during guided reading, the text Elizabeth was reading was leveled so carefully, she did not have as many opportunities to try to read words she did not know, and so her pattern of substitution without thinking about context went undetected. As a result of what she learned from examining Elizabeth's transcriptions, Vicki then spent time on reading lessons focused on using context clues to figure out unknown words or words students were not sure about as a result of her discovery about Elizabeth's reading processes. Even in Elizabeth's numerous miscues, Vicki noticed that many times Elizabeth retained the number of syllables the real word contained when she read them as nonwords. Examples of Elizabeth's miscues retaining the number of syllables include *spezzle* for *special*, *asdated* and *asdapted* for *adapted*, and *swecence* for *sequence*. Other times, Elizabeth substituted words she knew (real words) that looked similar to the printed text. Examples of these miscues include *mountains* for *maintain*, *couples* for *capable*, and *wolf's* for *whole*. Interestingly, all three of these miscues make sense when the context they were presented within is considered (the text being read is about wolves hunting for prey) showing that Elizabeth knows how to use context while reading; however, her miscues also show she does not check for meaning while reading. Here is an example of how she read the text when substituting "real" words she knows for what was written in the text:

mountains. (inserts period)
801 Wolves hunt with those in their pack and maintain this activity all

couples wolf's
802 year long. They are capable ~~of~~ spending a whole night hunting for

803 prey without ever taking a rest.

Another example occurred when Elizabeth substituted "made-up" words when she struggled with what was written in the text. Note from the miscues spelled above the words that she retains the syllables for two of the miscues but does not on one:

811 While following closely the tracks of a herd of deer, the wolves

® condinsun lanch
812 close in on the herd silently with coordination. Then, they launch

will be spreted
813 their attack. They try to separate the weakest deer from the

®groups
814 rest of the group.

Elizabeth's reading level was essentially incorrect when the formula was applied to more authentic texts associated with Accelerated Reader (AR) lists. This had repercussions because when Elizabeth self-selected books for AR, she typically chose those that other girls (more competent readers) were reading. These books, while in her prescribed reading range, were often too difficult for her because the vocabulary was not particularly controlled. She subsequently often failed AR tests required by the school. When her pattern of substituting words as meaningless placeholders emerged in RMA, Vicki found ways of effectively dealing with the problem, and her RMA group members also offered her support and strategies they used.

REFLECTION

Finding patterns of reading response leads to important discoveries about readers such as those for Vicki—patterns which she could easily mention in RMA groups for discussions and understanding. But another important reason for conducting RMA groups is the rich data collected to help a teacher make informed decisions about teaching reading in the classroom. The design of lessons are differentiated for every single student in the classroom, targeting skills that each student needs to improve in order to build capacity for comprehension, the reason for reading.

In this chapter, we see through readers' discussions what they know about reading. They know about chunking words, looking at roots, making connections to other words they know, and using resources. And in Elizabeth's case, she is learning about how important it is to make sense of text. The RMA discussions honored these students as readers and the skills they already had in place. In addition, of critical importance was the insight Vicki gained into what other kinds of instruction students needed to grow even stronger as readers.

8 RMA Conversations Focus the Classroom Literacy Curriculum

I think it's because she's thinking.

—Autumn, a third grader

This chapter will do the following:

- Show multiple miscue discussions students had that lead to identifying effective reading strategies
- Explain Retrospective Miscue Analysis (RMA) as a core approach to addressing multiple reading abilities in the literacy curriculum
- Use a sampling of retelling discussions to demonstrate student awareness of the depth of understanding during the reading process

THE MULTIPLICITY OF MISCUE CONVERSATIONS

RMA conversations are driven by the students in the group and center around the miscues that readers select for discussion. Without fail, the talk within the group focuses on a reading weakness or concern that again shows that students are quite aware of where their own reading skills break down or where they struggle in the reading process.

Confessions About Conventions

In this conversation among the developing readers, the students discussed the sentence ending omissions that Ron made during his recording. He ignores periods four times during the passage.

Ron: I'm used to reading longer sentences.

Phoenix: He corrects himself on line 204. He's kind of doing what I'm doing. He doesn't listen to the periods. I do that too. Sometimes that affects meaning.

Sentence ending punctuation is another subject of an RMA discussion with the striving readers. In the next example, Scott ignores a period, which creates a problem for reading of the next sentence.

ill. Fever burned her body. The doctors could not help. Her.

(ignores period; reads as if there is a period after her)

Vicki: I noticed that you ignored that period and made the period at the end of the line.

Jackson: The doctor could not help, well, could not help, could not help her makes sense.

Vicki: I could see why Scott did that. 'The doctors could not help her' makes sense. But then the next line doesn't make sense.

Scott: Was Helen Keller a real person?

Vicki: Helen Keller was a real person. She was a bit of a hero in our culture.

Scott: Was she really blind and deaf?

Vicki: Yes.

The ignored period miscue occurs again for Scott in the following dialogue. Abigail is thinking about the ignored miscue and thoughtfully makes a connection to what they have learned about sentence structure:

(ignores period)

Wanted to run and play But when she ran she crashed into trees

Abigail: I think I know why he ignored the period at the end of that sentence. We're not used to having *but* at the beginning of a sentence.

Vicki: I think you're right.

Using Words We Know to Figure Out New Words: Metacognition at Work

All of the prior work that students have done to prepare themselves for reading more difficult words, like chunking or finding a word we know within a word we do not know, showed up in miscue discussions. We also discovered another important insight in the following example. Nellie knows she has miscued, but she also knows that by continuing to read, she might be able to figure out what the word is, and she has confidence in herself as a reader as she continues to read further into the text. As Autumn notes in the opening quotation, the reader is "thinking" or metacognitively processing . . . thinking about what the reading means and building meaning to alternately predict and confirm the text.

Nellie: On line 707, I said *considerate* instead of *considered*. I think I just got those two confused. I knew the word *considered*, but I didn't know how it was spelled. So I just thought it was a different word. Then on the second miscue, 717, I recognized that word again, and I pronounced it correctly that time.

Vicki: Good, and that's what we want. That's what good readers do. The second or third time they see a word, they've got it in their brain; that's a great thing to notice.

Nellie: I knew it was a miscue. But I tried to do my best, and then the second time I knew what the word was.

Metacognition may be present for all readers, but those who are most proficient will utilize the act of thinking about what they are reading (Davenport, 1993) to build confidence in reading for comprehension.

Discussing New Vocabulary and Using Context Clues

In RMA discussions, it is easy for teachers to engage with in-the-moment teaching, or what Yetta Goodman (1996) calls critical moment teaching. During this particular session, the tape begins with Autumn reading. Kathie stops the tape to comment on a miscue, and Vicki seizes the opportunity to discuss a new vocabulary word all of the readers miscued on with this particular piece of text. It is also the perfect opportunity for Vicki to point out the similarities in the spelling of two words.

Kathie: She said *pincher*.

Vicki: She said *pinchers* instead of *pincers*. Do you know that word? It looks like pinchers, but pincers are more like little spears.

The example below also appears earlier in the book in a different context. In looking at it through a different lens, it is interesting to unveil what the students know about certain vocabulary words they have encountered during RMA and in other aspects of the classroom

Vicki: Integration is something that we talked about when we've talked about segregation.

Conrad: Integration is like when Martin Luther King joined the white and the black people to join hands.

Vicki: To stop segregation and to promote integration.

After listening to a tape recording by Jennie, the students have a discussion about one of her miscues, allowing a safe haven for her to discuss the rationale behind a miscue that obviously points out that she is not familiar with the word *launching*.

Vicki: Take a look at line 509. First she said *lounging*, then *lunging*, and then she said, *lunching*. What is she doing here?

Ron: Trying to find a word she knows to compare with *launching*?

508 The jumping spider's legs stretch the same way. But it hap-

lunching
lunging
lounging
509 -pens very fast, launching the spider into the air

Jennie: I'm not familiar with *launching*.

Notice in the transcript that follows, Vicki seizes an opportunity to reinforce the context clues strategies she has been teaching as a result of previous RMA sessions:

Vicki: Maybe we can figure out the meaning like we said before by looking at the words around it. Then you have learned a new vocabulary word!

Phoenix: Yeah, like "into the air."

Many mini-lessons about context clues had occurred previously; however, the RMA discussion that occurred with the following group was a more powerful lesson than any that Vicki could have created. Conrad is the reader and has miscued on the word *crevices* substituting *crack*.

Nellie: Think of a word like it that sounds different and sound it out.

Conrad: Like *crevices*. I just looked ahead at *crack*. I knew what it meant [crevices], but I couldn't pronounce it.

Vicki: Conrad gave a great example of use of context clues. He didn't know what a *crevice* was, but he looked back to *crack* and figured it out. There were also other clues he could have used like *goes between* and *rocks*.

Not only is this an excellent example of the use of context clues, but it demonstrates to readers that they consistently strive to make meaning from text. Conrad's brain was working hard to find a replacement for a word he was not comfortable pronouncing much like any speaker might do. It is another example of metacognition recognized during RMA conversations leading to stronger vocabulary development and fluency among group members. Without a doubt, the next time Conrad sees the word *crevice*, he will be able to both pronounce it and know the meaning!

Visualizing, Thinking Aloud, and Skimming

During the year we gathered information for this book, Vicki's students participated in a pilot program that explicitly teaches students about visualizing while reading. Visualizing is considered a powerful comprehension strategy, possibly because it is a natural part of the meaning making process (Moline, 1995). Vicki always struggled with program approaches to teaching, knowing an effective teacher looks for opportunities to use the information to be taught through meaningful, authentic discussion. And the impact of "practicing" visualizing while talking to students about the images they build in their heads while reading became evident throughout RMA sessions. In both of the discussions that follow, you will see Vicki reinforcing the concept of visualizing with two different RMA groups. First, the proficient readers:

Vicki: Do you think it's easier to draw pictures in your mind if it's fiction text?

All: Yeah!

Nellie: I had a picture of a starfish in my mind because they said it was related to the sea urchin. I didn't know if it really looked like it or not.

Next, the striving readers talk about visualizing while reading, but two other important strategies surface during the discussion—thinking aloud and skimming text:

Vicki: What pictures did you create in your mind?

Scott: Like if they're having a feast, I see the food.

Vicki: What about the buffalo stampede?

David: I take pictures in my mind, too.

Abigail: You can talk to yourself about what you're reading.

Jackson: I skim the pieces first.

One day the developing readers were having a discussion about words that give them trouble before the videotaping began. As Vicki set up the equipment, Phoenix talked about words that were unfamiliar to him. Ron offers this suggestion:

Ron: You could . . . before you even read the page, you could skim the page to make sure you know all the words.

Reading Fluency

Reading fluency has been discussed several times in our text. We revisit fluency here because once students hear themselves during RMA, they begin to correct fluency issues on their own. Earlier, we talked about Katie, a fifth-grade student in Vicki's classroom. She lacked confidence in reading aloud (something she wanted to improve on) and repeated during reading to the point of being a dysfluent reader. As RMA sessions began, Katie appeared to be extremely nervous during her first audiotaping session (it should be noted that the researcher was present for the first session to assist with operation of the recorder). She made 22 miscues during the first session. In subsequent tape recordings, Katie's miscues decreased.

The third grade students also discussed how repetitions affected reading fluency. Here is a discussion the third grade students had during an RMA session about repetitions that clearly shows how the brain works while reading:

Vicki: Nellie, why do you think you repeat a lot?

Autumn: I think it's because she's thinking.

Nellie: Probably because I like to read ahead so I might forget what I read so I go back and reread. And sometimes you stop and look around and forget where you are.

Making Connections

Text-to-text, text-to-self, and text-to-world connections (Keene & Zimmerman 1997, 2007) surface during RMA discussions. Making connections while reading and then discussing them during RMA is a powerful way to scaffold learning among peers. In the following discussion, Jennie has miscued *maniac* for *manage*. The group shows good humor when they laugh at the miscue, and Jennie joins in the laughter as well:

Jennie: I was thinking of *Maniac Magee* when I read that, so I thought it was maniac.

And here, it is interesting to note a comment from Ron when he pronounced *predector* much like *protector* and makes a text-to-life personal connection (Keene & Zimmerman, 1997, 2007) based on a miscued vocabulary word.

Ron: I think I said *predector* because my brother has to protect me a lot when we play video games.

Reading Different Kinds of Texts

As noted earlier, Vicki chose primarily to focus on reading nonfiction text during RMA sessions. By doing so, she taught the students about structural differences in text. The payoff was evident in discussion about differences between how we read fiction and nonfiction text and how those kinds of text "look" to the students. The conversation between Kathie and Conrad highlights this understanding:

Kathie: When you're reading nonfiction, you have more words in sentences.

Conrad: On lines 620 through 621, I skipped the periods because I'm used to longer words.

Kathie: Because when you're reading fiction, you could have 20 words in a sentence, but in nonfiction text you could have five or six words in a sentence.

Questioning the Author

One of the constants to come from miscue analysis research and in our own practice is that readers begin to question the author's writing style, especially if they notice the same miscue made by several readers. The preceding vignette is one example of this. We know readers are tuned into comprehending the text not sounding out every word when they start to make the kind of replacements that David made and the evaluation that Abigail makes when she says, "I think I would rather read it the way that David read it." We call this learning strategy "questioning the author." Use of the strategy develops a critical thinking skill that is taught in the reading curriculum (Vacca & Vacca, 2007); however, the original strategy does not provide the opportunity for readers to first "rewrite" the text and then explore the changes as RMA does, and quite effectively, as the readers above demonstrate.

Thinking Aloud

The Think Aloud strategy is often used by teachers to model the process of reading and transition children into successful silent reading habits. The strategy is versatile in that it may be used in both fiction and nonfiction text and is an excellent way to scaffold different patterns of text. During one Think Aloud opportunity in Vicki's classroom, the students are rereading a nonfiction text about the kinds of communities we live in. The text compares and contrasts suburban, urban, and rural communities. While the entire book is rich with photography, there are two pages of visual text (photographs) that are organized into a chart. The students did a thorough job of analyzing the photographs, seeing things Vicki had overlooked. To elicit further discussion, Vicki began "thinking aloud" after Jackson noted that in the urban shopping photo, there were "Chinese" people. She responded, "Yes, there are people of Asian descent in those pictures. I wonder in what kind of a market they are shopping?"

Vicki and her students continue the process in an effort to characterize their own community. Vicki again models the thinking aloud process saying, "I notice that you live in an area that is both suburban and rural. Why do I say that?" The students respond and because the students know that Vicki lives in an area of the city that contrasts with where they live, she continues the discussion. "What is different about where I live from where you live?" A student responds, "You can walk to the Dairy Queen or Subway. No fair!" They also note that she lives near the local university.

Try modifying the Think Aloud to show what you, as a mature reader, remember as you read "chunks" of the text or what you might have to go back and reread, which is a common "fix-up" strategy that struggling readers may not realize is useful during the entire reading process, not just afterwards, to answer comprehension questions.

Message Journals: "I am glad you are finding good books to read." —Ben's Mom

The discussions and explorations referred to throughout this book even crept into the students' journaling work in a triad between student, parents, and Vicki reiterating our belief in reading and writing as reciprocal processes, each one supporting the development of the other. For example, to expand upon Family Message Journals (Wollman-Bonilla, 2000) most of the students had participated in during their second-grade year. Vicki continued with the journals in third grade but in a slightly different way. Vicki felt as if the expanded curriculum in third grade would only allow journals to be completed three times a week rather than in a daily process. She also wanted to be a part of the journaling process with her students to gain information about how students were applying the learning from the classroom but also to find out how they felt about their reading and books in general. The students wrote to their parents Monday and Wednesday afternoons, and on Friday afternoon, they wrote to Vicki, giving her the weekend to write her responses.

The thoughtful conversations promoted through Socratic Circles are evident in a three-way journaling process among Ben, his mother, and Vicki. Integrating reading into social studies content, the students had been reading *Through My Eyes* by Ruby Bridges over a week-long study of the book. Ben writes to his mother:

> "Though [sic] My Eyes is about Ruby."

His mother responds to Ben:

> "I am glad you are finding good books to read. The story of Ruby is very good. When I worked in Mississippi in 1986, I think it was very sad that whites and blacks were still segregated. Do you know what segregated means?"

Then, Ben writes to Vicki:

> "Ruby Bridges sounds like the best gril [sic] in the world and so does Mrs. Henry sounds like best teacher like you Mrs. Seeger. Martin Luther King Jr. sounds good and sounds just like Ruby, Mrs. Seeger."

Vicki writes back to Ben:

> "Even though Ruby's story makes me very sad in parts, I think that it is important for us to continue to learn about her story. Even though things are better now than then, some parts of the United States are still difficult places for black people. Hard to imagine, isn't it? I am lucky to have a student like you who thinks about how others want to be treated."

EXPLORING OUR RETELLINGS TO ENHANCE MEANING

Jennie, Phoenix, Ron, Bastian, and Elizabeth are listening to their retelling sessions then discussing the similarities and differences in each one. In addition, Vicki tries to get the readers to explore strategies that will enhance their comprehension and understanding of the text. The group has just finished listening to Jennie's retelling of a piece of nonfiction text about spiders. The students in this group are what Vicki calls "average" readers. They are just getting used to doing retellings of text and their responses on the tape are somewhat limited. Vicki is trying to help them understand that a retelling is full and detailed and they must communicate that on tape.

Jennie's retelling is brief. She says, "I read about spiders and prey, and the story tells how jumping spiders catch their prey. There are amazing facts in the story I've never heard before."

Vicki: (To the group) Did she tell us the facts? Do I know she understands it?

All: No.

Jennie: I did understand.

Vicki: But did you tell enough on the retelling so we knew that?

Jennie: No, not enough.

The group listens to Elizabeth next whose retelling consists of one phrase: "I just read about a spider."

Vicki: From your retelling, do you think I would know if you understood what you read?

Elizabeth: No.

Vicki purposefully moves through each of the shallow retellings to illustrate a point to the students in the RMA session. Neither Jennie nor Elizabeth are very successful at their retelling, relying on one simple sentence to convey to the listener what they read about or giving a sentence containing an opinion, such as Jennie's. Bastian's retelling is next. He says, "I read how spiders jump and about their prey."

Phoenix: You can't really tell if he understood.

Jennie: He probably did, but if I hadn't read the same piece, I'd be confused about what it meant.

The group caught on to what Vicki is attempting to convey and quickly realized that Bastian's retelling is also lacking the details necessary to convey to someone else what the text is about.

Ron is next. He is a kind, sensitive boy who consistently reads quality literature, often seeking out the William Allen White Award books when he is selecting books for independent reading. He frequently wrote about what he was reading in his Family Message Journal and in his pen pal letters with preservice teachers, a project conducted with Rita's preservice reading course. Ron struggled when taking the AR tests on lengthy books he had read, although he could retell significant information from the books when asked. He was tearful and sad when he failed the literal answer seeking AR tests. During RMA, it is clear that Ron does comprehend text and focuses on the big picture rather than the minutiae often focused upon in the computerized tests.

Although Ron's fluency is by far the least developed of the group, his retelling is much stronger. He summarizes the story with four main points: "I read about a spider jumping on its prey. A spider is jumping and stretching its legs. I learned how far you can jump as a spider—25 times its body length. I read about how spiders inject poison into their prey."

Vicki: Who had the most information in their retelling?

All: Ron!

Vicki: What can we do to help remember what we read?

Phoenix: Reread?

Elizabeth: Read it again.

Vicki: Could you reread in a different way? What questions could you ask yourself to help you understand the piece when you read a second time?

Bastian: Skim it before you read it.

Jennie: Put it in your own words.

Vicki: Ron, how did you remember so many details like the spider jumping 25 feet?

Ron: I went back and put it in my own words and picked out some chunks of information.

Phoenix: I stop the tape and take a picture of what I'm reading in my mind.

While the readers did not respond to what Vicki was suggesting, they did come up with some useful and common strategies of their own. For example, they suggest rereading, skimming for information, chunking the information so that a summary sentence can be built from each chunk, and visualizing about the text. This RMA conversation explored how to better comprehend while reading using one of those strategies such as visualizing, to which Phoenix alludes. Vicki points this out to the students and validates all of their strategies as useful to understanding the text. Future retellings were much stronger after this RMA session confirming the success of a short, example-filled conversation demonstrated through audiotapes.

RMA AS THE CORE APPROACH TO ADDRESSING MULTIPLE READING ABILITIES IN THE LITERACY CURRICULUM

The use of RMA with younger readers is a relatively unexplored area of the research, especially the use of RMA as the core approach to teaching reading. Pahls-Weiss (2004) explored RMA with very young children in her work with selected readers in a first grade classroom. Martens' (1998) case study of a primary school student who benefited from the use of RMA paved the way for the use of RMA with younger children. Moore (Moore & Gilles, 2005) worked with a small group of fourth graders in a six-month study in RMA with a Title I teacher, and earlier with a third-grade student modeled on the work of Martens (1998). As far as Rita and Vicki can discern, whole-class instruction and the use of RMA in published work is limited to the middle school work of Costello (1996), the early work of Watson in Reader Selected Miscues (Watson, 1978) and later with Watson and Hoge (Watson & Hoge, 1996), as well as Rita's work with a high school language arts classroom in an alternative school setting in Kansas (Moore & Gilles, 2005).

When classroom spaces for readers who struggle provide safe and welcoming environments, then conversations like the examples provided readily take place. The label given these readers, *striving*, does not nearly describe the intensity and complexity of their insights. Rita visited Vicki's classroom several times during the RMA work with the third graders. One of the things she had trouble keeping straight was which group was supposed to be proficient and which was striving because their conversations were *all* rich and insightful. They were all refining strategies such as "questioning the author" and discussing eye movement related to reading—the kinds of things Rita was introducing to her university students—the topics that linguists and reading specialists often discuss.

In addition, the skills learned during RMA sessions spill over into other classroom contexts such as the development of purposeful and critical listening skills evidenced in all of the RMA groups as well as in the outer Socratic Circles where listening was key to success. Many of the strategies discussed in this chapter apply to teaching and learning across the curriculum. Content reading took on another dimension, explored through the reading miscues of the children as they continuously made connections to previously read text or writings in their journals.

REFLECTION

This chapter came to fruition after a recent discussion Rita and Vicki had while working on other chapters. As we talked about how to complete the book, Vicki began reminiscing about how much she had learned from implementing RMA first, and then Socratic Circles with this group of third-grade students. Over and over again, she cited strategies the students had applied and talked expertly about during RMA discussions. As we looked at the transcripts once again, it became clear that RMA, not guided reading, was the arena where we learned what strategies students were employing to access and make sense of the text they were reading. RMA was also the place where Vicki was easily able to reinforce the learning occurring from other instructional programs in a meaningful, productive way.

9 Socratic Circles and RMA

And these third-grade learners really took it seriously!

—Vicki

This chapter will do the following:

- Explain the history and structure of Socratic Circles
- Examine three concepts central to both Retrospective Miscue Analysis (RMA) and Socratic Circles
- Describe Socratic Circle technique as a path to implementing whole-class RMA
- Examine the parallels between Socratic Circles and RMA
- Explore how to teach critical listening skills with RMA and Socratic Circles

THE HISTORY AND NATURE OF SOCRATIC CIRCLES

Socratic Circles are established with the intent that the members of the entire group will benefit from what they hear in small group discussions. Vicki, for example, realized that the students needed work on listening to one another—not a strength of young students all yearning to be heard at the same time, and she needed a process to better facilitate listening and observation skills. The nature and philosophy of Socratic Circles is grounded in the development of critical listening skills as well as the ability to learn how to provide constructive feedback to others. Vicki had experienced Socratic Circles (Copeland, 2005) earlier in Rita's graduate class and recalled the strengths of the process in that setting. She was impressed with the high-level discussion that resulted with peers in her graduate course, and she began asking, why not alter the experience for use with younger students in a format they could easily understand?

Socratic Circle technique stems from the dialogues the ancient Greek philosopher Socrates engaged in with his students and documented through their writings. It provides a systematic method for involving all students in a dialogic process in the classroom where the learning is honored and connected to prior knowledge. It is an especially useful format for involving every student in a high-level discussion that takes the teacher out of the role of asking all the questions and puts students in a place where they can critically think about a subject or concept along with their peers (Copeland, 2005).

THREE CONCEPTS UNDERLYING RMA AND SOCRATIC CIRCLES

There are three concepts underlying the use of RMA and Socratic Circles. The first is empowerment: RMA strategies combined with Socratic Circle technique empower all readers and build a sense of community in the classroom. RMA essentially represents small group reading conversations about graphophonic, syntactic, semantic, or pragmatic miscues of language.

Socratic Circle technique provides a supplemental process that supports the implementation of RMA. Socratic Circles are composed of an outer circle of "observers" who explore the reading process by listening to the RMA group members discuss their miscues of pronunciation and meaning. The outer circle members later constructively share observations with the inner circle; the roles are then reversed in subsequent reading sessions.

The second concept is the relationship between literacy and language learning: the interpretation of miscues by the readers during RMA provides a vital source of learning about language and literacy. Chapter 4 shows how miscue analysis can be adapted for classroom teachers and their students.

RMA empowers children to understand that all readers are "working" toward making sense from text by drawing on knowledge, experience, culture, and the language around them. RMA conversations offer the teacher valuable insight into how children use their knowledge of language and literacy to understand the printed word. We believe that all readers work at reading text for meaning even though levels of reading proficiency may range from one type of text to another. For example, one might read narrative text as a proficient reader but a physics text as a striving reader. The same concept is at work in our classrooms, but often readers do not understand that they have the capability of becoming proficient.

The third concept is building community through access: given equitable opportunities for discussion, the conversations about miscues and retellings may be equally rich among all levels of reading proficiency. For example, even with the readers who struggled the most, the RMA conversations about their miscues and retellings were as insightful as those of the readers who were more proficient. Each group learned from the other; each were engaged in similar learning processes, the outcomes of which were grounded in what they knew or discovered about language as individuals and as groups. Whether as RMA discussants or Socratic observers, each participant was engaged in the discussion, respectful of others, and truly invested in the process of finding out how reading works. Visitors to Vicki's classroom were amazed at the level of community, maturity, and commitment to the process demonstrated by the third graders, characterized by other teachers as "a challenging, diverse class" both academically and in terms of management.

SOCRATIC CIRCLES AS A PATH TO WHOLE-CLASS RMA

An inkling that Socratic Circles just might work in the elementary classroom came as Vicki worked with her fifth-grade students the previous year. The four students engaged in RMA that year initially began the process of completing all the tasks associated with RMA "in private." Tape recording occurred in a private area (actually a large closet that became a part of the classroom work areas), and RMA sessions were held while other students were out and about in the first-grade classroom with Book Buddies. But, as the process continued and the four students became increasingly more comfortable with RMA, the sessions were held while other students were engaged in writing workshop or reading response tasks.

The group representing Vicki's most competent readers were very curious and paid close attention to the RMA sessions. They were clearly intrigued and desired to have a similar experience. One day, Vicki asked them to discuss how they learned to be such competent readers, and she videotaped their discussion. It was a powerful discourse that Vicki shared with Rita, who then shared it with her university students, who were completely amazed at the depth of discussion. From this tape, we learned that these children were quite capable of critically analyzing what reading is, how it is acquired, including giving their home and preschool experiences credit for their early reading acquisition and love of books. It became clear to Vicki that through observation of the initial reading group about reading tasks and discussion, another group, who were much more proficient readers, learned about dialoguing about the reading process via a small group discussion. We decided that Socratic Circles were possible with younger students.

The idea that Socratic Circles could be a powerful discussion strategy was solidified during Vicki's fifth-grade classroom the year before. After two of many fifth-grade classroom discussions when vivid dialogue occurred about complex science topics—Newton's First Law of Physics and how our universe was formed—Vicki began holding discussions in circular groupings with everyone facing the middle to promote eye contact, creating a powerful dynamic of social interaction. All desks were pushed to the sides of the classroom, and Vicki and the students sat on the floor to hold important, lengthy discussions often lasting 30 to 40 minutes (not by lesson design, but by virtue of the depth and meaning-making occurring). An easel with a chart paper poster sat at one end of the circle with the norms for group discussion and a reminder to think about connections—student schema that might assist others to develop meaning. In addition, students took turns facilitating the discussion taking Vicki out of leading the discussion. The facilitator's "duties" were to be certain everyone was heard, bring discussion back to the intent if the group strayed from topic, and signal the easel if the group was not valuing the norms. Vicki videotaped the discussions and was struck by the in-depth dialogue that occurred. In reflecting upon these videotapes, she realized that, indeed, processes like Socratic Circles could work with younger students.

PARALLELS BETWEEN SOCRATIC CIRCLES AND RMA

The way we experience the world is based on our previous experiences. And any thinking we do is based on prior thinking and paves the way for future thinking. So it is that any thought or idea we have "can be further developed and better explained" (Copeland, 2005, p. 8). In Socratic Circles, students are encouraged to further develop their thinking about some topic. Using Socratic Circles with RMA is logical, as students begin to make sense of the reading processes and how they react with text. Just like Socratic Circles, RMA allows students to further their thinking about reading, specifically.

Copeland (2005) writes about the skills that students develop while engaged in Socratic Circles, including critical thinking skills. In most classrooms, the students are focused on answering teacher-led discussion questions where the expectation is that a correct response will be given. Copeland notes that two other scenarios often occur: an incorrect response or the student simply says, "I don't know the answer." In Socratic Circles and RMA, the focus upon correct responses is removed as students involve themselves in a discussion that revolves around pieces of the content that are important to them. Too much reading instruction today leaves students with little or no voice about what is discussed. Vicki and Rita both note that in all of their RMA sessions with students, no student has ever uttered, "I don't know," when talking about miscues and retelling content.

Another benefit of Socratic Circles is development of critical reflection skills, involving "mulling over past experiences, assessing one's own performance, and establishing goals for future performance" (Copeland, 2005, 18–19). In RMA, students are able to reflect on their past reading experiences when they look at their miscues over time. It is not unusual to hear a student say, "I did that last time I read!" Students participate in assessment of their reading performance by thinking about whether the miscue is of a high level, and thus not changing the meaning, or whether the miscue is low level and affected the meaning of the text. And perhaps, most important, the students are able to establish goals for themselves related to their future reading performance.

IMPLEMENTING AND MANAGING SOCRATIC CIRCLES AND RMA

We will explain how to modify the original Socratic Circle process presented by Copeland (2005) for high school and middle school students to better fit the developmental needs of younger readers. We modify the process by framing it within the context of reading instruction, whereas Copeland frames the process primarily through critical inquiry into philosophical discussion of content. Even though the process is modified, the RMA and Socratic outcomes of rich language experiences, constructing meaning from text, motivating and improving critical literacy skills, and building classroom community remain the same.

The rationale behind the use of Socratic Circles is to provide a venue that ensures the entire class benefits from all of the RMA conversations and to "level the playing field" so that differences in reading ability do not focus the classroom perception of reading and readers. The emphasis of the combined approach of RMA and Socratic Circles to teach reading is on exploring the nuances of meaning of text, exploring language and language processes through talk (Barnes, 1975/1992), and building classroom community through Socratic Circles (Copeland, 2005).

In Vicki's class, Socratic Circles were conducted about once a month. During these intervals, the class observed and listened to each of the RMA discussion groups, then commented on what they had observed in respectful, constructive ways. While Vicki grouped the children in flexible ability groups, the same procedures were followed for RMA by each group, allowing insight and thoughtful responses to be recognized rather than pronunciation errors or "getting all the answers right" on the retelling.

Socratic Circles are organized with two circles of students: an inner circle and an outer circle. The purpose is to involve the entire class as a community of readers recognizing strengths and reading behaviors of their peers. Students in the inner circle are members of a single RMA group. This may be a high, middle, or lower reading group. The rest of the class functions as the outer circle. The students in the outer circle are charged with listening to the RMA conversation and taking notes on (1) how well the participants are communicating with one another and (2) the context of their conversation. They are provided with a Socratic Circles Tracking Sheet (Resource I) to guide their focused listening. As always, RMA group members are provided with the marked Simplified Miscue Organizer that helps them focus their conversations. When the inner circle is finished with their RMA conversation, they listen quietly to the comments from the outer circle. Then they may respond and comment, and a full class conversation may ensue. Socratic Circles seemed to be a reasonable way to facilitate meaningful group discussions as a class about what was being said during selected RMA sessions. And it is a good tool to model what we expect from students during discussions in the classroom. Socratic Circles were held once a month with RMA groups. How to set up the process for RMA group discussion is defined below, drawing on specific examples from Vicki's experiences.

Step 1: Setting the Stage

Choose a few students to model the RMA group conversations that would be observed by members of the Socratic Circle. Vicki explained the Socratic Circle process whereby one RMA group (five students and Vicki) would sit in chairs arranged in a circle, play the recorded reading while following along with transcribed miscues (now in their folders), and discuss the miscues that occurred. As in writing workshop prior to the day of implementation, Vicki asked two students if their tape recordings and miscue recording sheets could be used during Socratic Circles. Each agreed. Vicki purposefully chose Autumn as one of the models, a very bright and articulate student but often overlooked by her peers because she takes longer than most to formulate her words and then speak. The Socratic Circles process, in a way, "forced" her peers to be patient and wait on Autumn's insightful words.

Next, the remainder of the students (nine) stood behind and surrounded the small RMA group. The standing students were instructed to use their observation and listening skills to reflect on what occurred during the RMA discussion. Copeland (2005) notes the importance of having the inner and outer circles at different levels so that the outer circle has a full view of the inner circle by looking over them as they proceed in the process. Using clipboards, paper, and pencil, they could take notes on their Tracking Sheet or simply listen. After the RMA group's discussion ended, they would be invited to tell what they had observed, suggest any improvements that were needed, and constructively talk about specific reading and interactive behaviors of the group. These were abbreviated RMA sessions intended to provide the class practice in conducting RMA and Socratic Circles jointly.

Step 2: Laying the Ground Rules for Discussion and Socratic Comments

In Chapter 5, we discussed laying the ground rules for RMA conversations. The same ground rules can be modified for Socratic Circles as the children in the outer circle listen to and observe the RMA conversation of the inner circle. Review with the outer circle the ground rules for RMA prior to beginning Socratic Circles, especially the notion that miscues are not "mistakes," rather, they are responses to text based on the expectations of the reader. Advise the students to think about the conversation they are observing in "miscue" terms so that the discussion remains focused on language and reading process rather than on how much the reader knows or how many errors are made.

This procedure and mindset is especially important to establish during the first Socratic Circles. The outer circle should be instructed to jot down the miscues and reactions to the retellings they hear and then respond to the questions listed in Step 3 when it is their turn to comment. It is helpful if the teacher asks the outer circle for a list of the miscues they heard from each reader, comments on the retellings they would like to make, and then frames the discussion with the five RMA questions (repeated below in Step 3) from Chapter 5, adding the sixth for Socratic Circles.

Resource I provides a reproducible Socratic Circles tracking sheet that may help the outer circle remain focused on readers and examples of the reading and language processes they hear "in action" during the RMA conversation.

Step 3: Getting Started

The audiotape was played as students in the inner circle followed along with the coded miscues. Those in the *outer circle* also had copies of the coded miscues they would hear discussed. This modeled the RMA procedure students used at each future session and clearly set the stage for expectations to follow. Students in the *inner circle,* the RMA group, followed RMA procedures in which they were invited to stop the audiotape at any point to discuss a particular miscue. The miscues were talked about within the RMA group with the reader always being offered the first opportunity to comment on what prior knowledge or experiences may have influenced them to miscue. The seven key questions, five of which were referred to first in Chapter 5 were posted to guide the observations of the outer circle as well as the conversation of the inner circle (part of the usual RMA process).

1. Did the miscue change the meaning of the sentence?
2. What does the miscue tell us about what the reader knows about language?
3. What was the reader thinking at the time the miscue was read?
4. What kinds of connections was the reader making?
5. What prior knowledge does the reader have that might have helped him or her understand the text?

We have added two questions since Chapter 5 for Socratic Circles that help capture the importance of the retelling and how retellings often reveal a great deal about comprehension and reading processing.

6. Was the miscue a "smart" or an "okay" miscue?
7. What did you notice about the retelling that gives you more information about how the reader made meaning of the text?

Step 4: Learning From the Outer Circle

Interestingly, Vicki's expectation that students would have little to say during this first session was proven incorrect; students had plenty to say, including both the inner circle and the outer circle. Thinking that the outer circle would focus on student behaviors (third graders are skilled at noticing what others are doing), Vicki was surprised when they talked about miscues! They noticed that the reader did not use "voice" when she read; however, the group concluded that using voice was not always important for understanding the text. They also noticed who had remained quiet during the RMA discussion.

A key element of Socratic Circles is that the teacher does not interfere with student discussion, empowering students to construct knowledge on their own. Because RMA conversations were just beginning, Vicki was compelled to facilitate during the process but pleasantly surprised at how little she had to speak during the initial sessions. The only reminders needed during the session were that, just like any other classroom discussion, it was not necessary to raise hands, but students needed to respect one another's comments and allow that person to finish before someone else spoke.

Vicki attributed the success of the beginning RMA sessions to carefully leading the class through the outlined procedures above, including facilitating the procedures associated with Socratic Circles. Socratic Circles provided a way to let students know what was going to go on before they came to an RMA session. Being nervous about RMA procedures was limited and only seemed to affect one student, Nellie, but she was able to acknowledge this and talk about it during an initial session. The following is a discussion that occurred about Nellie's confusion while trying to conduct a retelling on a passage about Rosa Parks (Bridges, 1999) during Socratic Circles:

Nellie: Usually when I listen to myself on tape . . . I always . . . when I know people are going to listen to me, I always get nervous. I forget what I'm going to say. My palms start to sweat.

Vicki: We're all feeling kind of nervous about this. But Nellie, it's okay to say you're confused (referring to her earlier statement in this discussion about being confused during retelling). If we weren't asking you to do a retelling about what you had just read, you would go back, reread it, think about it again, and you're not going to reread it in the same way again, are you?

All: No.

Vicki:	No, you have to ask yourself some new questions before you do that.
Autumn:	I think she understood, she just couldn't say it.
Nellie:	I look at the details about how she was treated and how people thought of her.
Vicki:	Did you understand those parts?
Nellie:	Yes, I did.

The following is a list of direct quotations taken from the first combined RMA and Socratic Circle Session. The readers in this session gave these reasons for miscues noted by those in the inner circle.

- "Because it looks that way."
- "They are similar." (*onto* and *into*)
- "Same letters in a different order."
- "Smart miscue—substitution."
- "Switched letters in the word." (*spots* and *stops*)

The outer circle of students was allowed to discuss the session only after the inside group was finished. In addition to identifying some of the explanations for the miscues, one student in the outer circle noted that the reader did not use "voice" when that particular reader read. But the group concluded that using voice was not always important for understanding the text. The listeners in the outer group also note the following as helpful in understanding some of the inner circle miscues and agreed that many times they used some of the same strategies as the inner circle when reading.

- Word begins the same but ends differently. (*pretend* and *predator*)
- Forming a contraction was a smart miscue because it "shortens it up."
- Omitting a sentence ending was a smart miscue because we are "used to longer sentences when we read."

The foundation for Socratic Circles is similar to that of RMA conversations: valuing the contributions of a group through the eyes of the whole. The idea is to establish an atmosphere within the classroom community where learners may safely express and explore their miscues, the meanings behind them, and the multiple connections the readers may make to the text.

There were outcomes both similar and distinct within and across the effects of RMA on the readers in Vicki's classroom. Developmental differences emerged in how the various students responded to conversations about oral reading miscues, their retellings, their interaction styles, and their newfound strengths and challenges as readers. Discussions around these differences as a result of Socratic Circle intervals contributed to a stronger learning community. For example, when hearing the proficient readers' heart-to-heart discussion about their own retelling, Nellie was confident to reveal things about herself as a reader she never did before. Prior to the use of Socratic Circles and RMA in Vicki's classroom instruction, Nellie's discussions always took on a silly, self-deprecating quality. It is important to note that the retellings being compared are Kathie's and Conrad's, but all of the readers offer insight into retellings because they feel safe to do so.

Vicki: What did you notice about Conrad's retelling?

Kathie: He told more details about the story than he read.

Vicki: He told more details. When you're doing a retelling, and you want someone to really understand you . . . .

Kathie: You should do that (meaning every reader should do that).

(Vicki smiles at Kathie's quick understanding and asks why.)

Kathie: Well, if not, you'd wonder what the story was really about and why are we listening to it.

Vicki: What differences did you notice, Kathie, in your telling and Conrad's? How could you have changed your retelling to help me as a teacher better understand your retelling?

Kathie: I could have put more details in and compared what I understood and did not understand.

Autumn: I noticed he (Conrad) had more details. . . .

Nellie: I noticed that in mine, I didn't tell too much about what I was reading. Conrad told us more about the story . . . what he understood.

Vicki: I noticed that all of you included more about the beginning of the text rather than the end. Why do you think you did that?

Kathie: I think it's because we understood the top part more than the bottom. In the bottom there were bigger words like *surrounding* and *crevices*.

Nellie: I think I pretty much understood the story. It's just when I mispronounce a few word so then I won't understand that word and the next together. I always remember the top better

> than the bottom. When I read the bottom, it didn't stick to my memory as much as the top does. I didn't read it quite as fast, either.

Just as with the RMA conversation participants, the members of the Socratic Circle are not focused on correcting errors. Comments and discussions from Socratic Circles demonstrate that the children focus on the analysis of miscues and retellings in addition to how the readers participated in the discussions. For example, in one Socratic Circles session, the outer circle talked about the inner circle's discussion about being confused while reading. Autumn acknowledges what the others are feeling and experiencing and that those in the inner circle are " . . . sort of like me. I know what I want to say in my head, but it's hard to get it out in words."

Socratic Circle technique may be used to observe and comment on the RMA reading groups, thus extending greater independence in critical literacy through reading conversations within the entire class. Teachers will notice nuances to suggest when the lines between the "proficient," "developing," and "striving" reading groups diminish and how to use that effect to build greater classroom community that goes beyond the reading curriculum.

TEACHING CRITICAL LISTENING SKILLS: RMA AND SOCRATIC CIRCLES

Certain skills that emerge from readers learning to "speak RMA" may spill over in other classroom activities such as cooperative learning groups and guided reading where respectful and constructive conversation is key to the success of the learning activity. Listening skills are particularly difficult to teach to young children but are often a required component of a school district's literacy curriculum. RMA coupled with Socratic Circles is an authentic and meaningful way to teach listening skills. The two strategies provide children with a purpose for listening and then critically and constructively evaluating information. The use of Socratic Circles presented a unique opportunity for Vicki to involve the entire class in reading discussions. Unlike guided reading groups where only small-group interaction is shared, the introduction of Socratic Circles allowed the examination of all of the RMA groups' interactions.

Vicki has been reading *Through My Eyes* by Ruby Bridges (Bridges, 1999) to the students. Following Socratic Circle technique, the inner circle RMA group is discussing the section of text she has just read aloud to them while the rest of the class forms an outer circle to listen and take notes. In the next dialogue examples are comments and discussion first from the RMA group and then from the outer Socratic Circle that demonstrate the powerful interactions teachers might expect from these combined learning strategies.

What began as a book that had a cheerful looking cover with a smiling child on it quickly turns serious and somber as the text is read, and the RMA group begins to discuss:

Ron: It is so sad that the adults treated Ruby that way and that she couldn't even play with the other kids in the school.

Autumn: It would be awful to have to be by yourself all day. And then the white people outside the school said they were going to poison Ruby's lunch. She's afraid to eat her lunch.

Phoenix: Ruby didn't do anything to anyone. She's just a little girl.

Jackson: At least she had Mrs. Henry.

Phoenix: But that's not the same as getting to play with kids.

After the discussion of the inner circle ended, the outer circle had their turn. The following are representative responses from the outer circle that had just finished listening to and taking notes on the RMA conversation.

Bastian: Everything they said is what I was thinking. It reminds me of that other girl we talked about.

Bastian is talking about Linda Brown, one of the subjects of the *Brown vs. Board of Education* decision in 1954. The students are familiar with the story of the young girl from their own city of Topeka, Kansas, who was forced to walk to a bus stop to catch a bus to the "black" school a long way from her home, past the "white" elementary school in her own neighborhood. In the next quotation, Kathie picks up on another part of the book that the RMA group missed, thus adding to the richness of the discussion.

Kathie: Yeah, but Ruby was even younger than that girl. They (the inner circle) did a good job discussing, but they didn't talk about the part of the book we read yesterday. About Ruby and her mom sitting in the school office all day long. That's just wrong!

To help teachers obtain a visual understanding of how Socratic Circles are set up, we have included two diagrams. The first, Figure 9.1, shows the arrangement of students in the inner and outer circle, and the second, Figure 9.2, demonstrates the teacher's movements to facilitate progress in both groups.

Figure 9.1 Arrangement of Students in Inner and Outer Circle

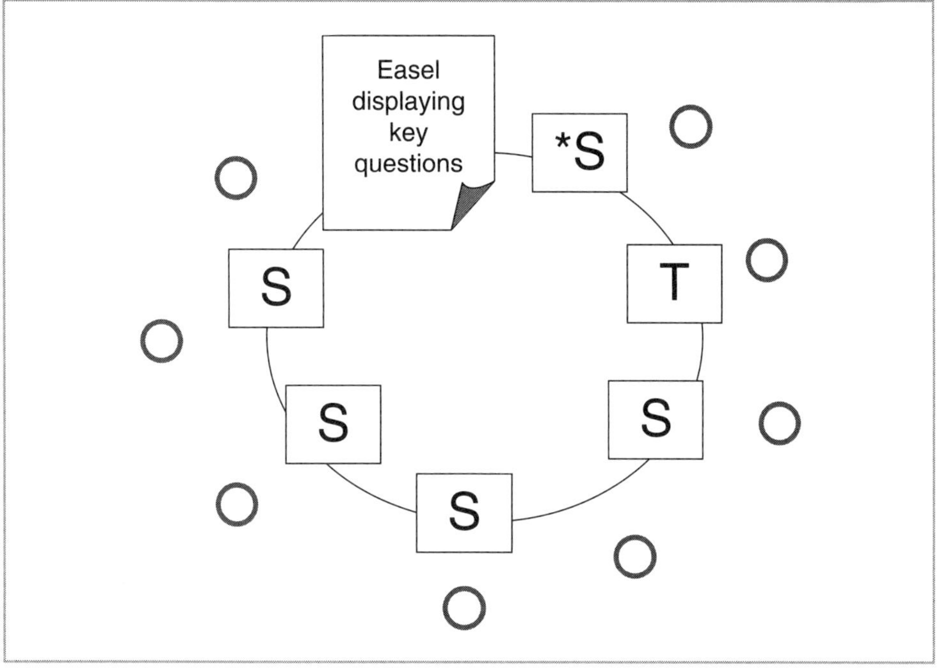
Easel displaying key questions
*S
S
T
S
S
S

Key to Figure 9.1: S = Students in inner circle; * denotes student holding tape recorder; T = Teacher; O = Observers in outer circle.

Figure 9.2 Teacher's Movements to Facilitate Progress

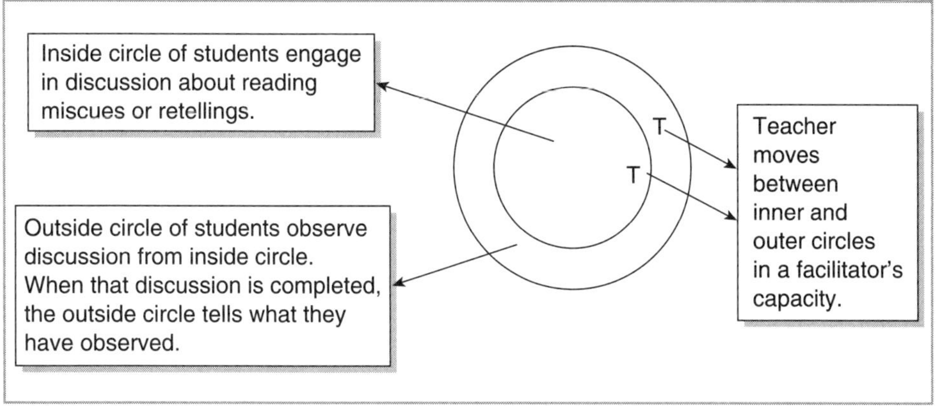
Inside circle of students engage in discussion about reading miscues or retellings.
Outside circle of students observe discussion from inside circle. When that discussion is completed, the outside circle tells what they have observed.
T
T
Teacher moves between inner and outer circles in a facilitator's capacity.

REFLECTION

The addition of Socratic Circles allowed whole-class participation and formally recognized and encouraged the development of young children's critical inquiry into the reading process. In fact, based on our experiences with the children, we recommend using Socratic Circles early in the school year to facilitate building a community of respectful and thoughtful listeners and learners. Socratic Circle technique effectively frames RMA conversations and allows their results to be shared within a safe, structured process that builds classroom community.

The rationale for using Socratic Circles underscores the rationale for RMA: building trust and empowering learners to think critically and with the understanding that there may be more than one "correct" response when reading and that each reader processes text individually based on prior knowledge and experiences. The use of Socratic Circles builds an articulate community of learners who come together with the purpose of learning from one another. In Vicki's words, "And these third-grade learners really took it seriously!"

Socratic Circles leveled the playing field for all readers of all abilities in that each RMA group was observed and listened to using the same ground rules and questions. Examples show how there was no reference to high, middle, or low reading groups by the outer circles, and since the make-up of the outer circle involved a mixture of ability levels, their perspectives brought a new richness toward understanding the reading process in action. What worked for readers and what did not, as well as examining—much as one examines a puzzle or problem analytically and systematically—the experiences, knowledge of language, and connections to other readings that might affect individual readings and retellings were all made evident.

In Chapters 10, 11, and 12, we will show how RMA with Socratic Circle technique benefited all of the ability groups: proficient, developing, and striving. We will present representative examples of literacy strategies and skills that emerged from the various groups that often penetrated other aspects of the curriculum and classroom learning community as well.

10 RMA and Proficient Readers

I've never heard of that word in my life.

—Nellie, a third grader

> This chapter will do the following:
>
> - Discuss the importance of including proficient readers in the classroom reading community
> - Demonstrate how the vitality of cooperative group work comes to life during Retrospective Miscue Analysis (RMA)

INCLUDING EFFECTIVE AND PROFICIENT READERS AS MODELS FOR THE CLASSROOM READING COMMUNITY

Effective and proficient readers are sometimes overlooked when establishing reading instruction; teachers naturally tend to focus on how to reach struggling readers. The focus on struggling readers promoted by Reading First has left many skilled readers to their own devices for furthering their knowledge about their own reading skills and behaviors and about literature. How to use RMA to support effective and proficient readers will be explained through a series of modified miscue analyses followed by RMA conversation sessions among the children.

Conrad, Nellie, Autumn, and Kathie comprised Vicki's highest ability reading group. They quickly compared their work in RMA groups to their coveted book club meetings.

One might ask, why put effective readers into RMA groups? The answer lies in the power of the RMA process to help *all* readers learn to think about reading as a socially rich language event rather than the task of simple reading and decoding. Even though readers may be proficient, their responses during RMA are sometimes surprising. They often enlighten themselves and others about the reading process, the thinking behind the miscues or retelling, and they become excellent critics of writing style and text. When their thoughts become overt during the whole-class activity of Socratic Circles, the knowledge and discoveries are shared across the classroom community.

We were often struck by how the students appear so businesslike in their RMA discussions, seeking clarification when they do not understand another student's thinking. The RMA process allows for in-depth discussions not seen in regular guided reading groups focused more on correcting mistakes rather than understanding why the miscue may have occurred in the first place, or how the retelling might be enriched by further contemplation of the author's purpose or meaning. The RMA "talk" by these proficient readers is reminiscent of adult literature discussions, and the teacher is a full participant in the discussion, no longer a facilitator. Teachers gain insight into these readers at a level not possible through less organic, skills-based processes like guided reading.

BUILDING COOPERATIVE LEARNING GROUPS

Besides serving as an effective method for teaching reading, RMA provides a positive and effective cooperative group activity, particularly for younger readers who may have never before been given significant responsibility for understanding their own reading processes. For example, the severe disruptive behaviors demonstrated in Vicki's classroom by one student in the proficient group completely disappeared during RMA. The student functioned at a high level and contributed particularly insightful comments, showing her capability for empathic and sophisticated responses to her peers—behaviors that were rarely seen in other classroom settings. Had she not been a part of an RMA group, Vicki might never have known that this child was capable of functioning at such an appropriate and socially acceptable level.

Because of the careful preparation and groundwork laid through the Socratic Circles process, the students came to the RMA sessions fully prepared to work on their reading skills by (1) allowing all participants to present their audiotape in their own way by stopping and starting the tape at miscues important to each person, (2) contributing respectful comments about reading miscues, (3) offering plausible reasons for the miscues, and (4) processing the content of retellings within the group. A fifth "byproduct" of this process occurred when students began using their RMA and Socratic Circles at other times in classroom discussions.

Developing Vocabulary

Students knew what miscues they wanted to focus on, especially after RMA was well under way. About a month into classroom RMA conversations, repetitions and self-corrections were often ignored and students instead chose miscues that held deeper or personal meaning for them, much like the unfamiliar word Nellie refers to as never having heard in her life.

Word Similarities, Differences, and Connecting to Other Text

We will now explore some of the conversations and outcomes heard with the proficient readers. The conversation in this group concentrates on similarities and differences in word configurations as well as possible connections to previously read text. Kathie explains the repetition, noting that readers predict ("read ahead") and confirm ("go back and repeat.").

The children are reading from *Lewis and Clark and Me* (Meyers, 2002), which is narrated from the camp dog, Seaman's, point of view. Vicki facilitated the discussion, but students were reminded that during RMA, no hands need to be raised, but students need to respect all participant comments (allowing each other to finish). As they listened to Conrad's tape and discussed his miscues, the following conversation ensued:

Conrad: It looks like *crops* (*corps*). The *o* and *r* are mixed up. It is an okay miscue.

Conrad: *Clearing* looks like *cleaning*.

Kathie: They are very similar.

Kathie: He repeated tough words, tough sentences. Some periods, he just ignored.

Autumn: *Though* looks like *thought*.

Nellie: *Here* and *there* are the same things.

Kathie: He repeated on line 319.

Autumn: Maybe he was thinking or lost track of where he was.

Conrad: Was it something out of his journal (William Clark)?

Kathie: He was changing gears. Maybe he was reading ahead and then had to go back and repeat.

Autumn: I do that. Sometimes, I read the end of the book.

Next, the group listened to Nellie's tape. Nellie had three miscues, so there was little discussion; however, there is an important connection made:

Conrad: Nellie used a lot of voice when she read.

Kathie: I noticed that she read *four dogs* after *four horses*. I can understand why she did that, but if I didn't know about Seaman being the only dog, it would make a difference. It's an okay miscue.

Again, Kathie demonstrated understanding of the miscue that occurred—the *why*—but she also explained why it affected meaning, making it an okay miscue.

The following discussion is about Rosa Parks, integration, and segregation. It would have been easy for the discussion to become stalled or deteriorate because of misunderstanding the text. The teacher's role is a constant pulling back and moving in only when needed—scaffolded support at its best.

More Insights and Connections

In another session with proficient readers who generally do not struggle on most text, more insights and connections develop during the RMA conversation. Notice how Vicki tries to help the readers understand what may have influenced their miscues.

Vicki: Take a look at Kathie's miscues. I noticed that there are a few places where she had difficulty with hyphenated words just like the rest of us did. Did anybody notice that?

Conrad: Yea, I noticed on line 705, she put "innnn . . . ." What's it say?

Vicki: Well, she read *integrated*, which would make sense for this piece, but the word is *ignited*. She eventually says *ignited*.

The group giggles.

Vicki: Integration is something that we talked about when we've talked about segregation.

Conrad: Integration is like when Martin Luther King joined the white and the black people . . . to join hands.

Vicki: To stop segregation and to promote integration. And it's understandable that you thought that word was *integration*. Later, she says *concerned* for *considered*.

What do you think about that?

Autumn: They look the same. They both start with *c-o-n*, and then the *c* sounds like the *s*.

Vicki: One of the things I noticed on your [Kathie's] text, you read really, really fast. And that can affect how we understand it. We can maybe not be as careful when we read fast, so one of the things I would encourage you to do is to slow down.

Autumn: One thing I noticed is that she . . . like she read the whole thing repeating.

Vicki: Is repetition a bad thing?

Autumn: No.

Vicki: Not unless we do it all the time. How does it help us?

Kathie: It helps us understand what we're talking about.

Vicki: Why do we repeat?

Nellie: Uh . . . like in *The Hundred Penny Box,* sometimes the words don't make sense, but when I reread, it dings in my head what it's saying.

Conrad: Like something like . . . I can't remember . . . Pontiac tree . . . something . . .

Vicki: So there is some vocabulary in *The Hundred Penny Box* that you're not familiar with, plus it is in the dialect of the South. I am so glad that you're making a connection between what you're reading in guided reading and what we're doing here in CRMA. All of these things help us make sense of our reading. When you start making text-to-self, text-to-text, or text-to-world connections, you become a better reader. I think the only miscue I wanted to discuss with Kathie is her last one. Kathie, what did you think about that miscue?

Kathie: I read *challenges* for *changes*. Because they pretty much look the same.

Vicki: Well they do, but I am thinking you did it for another reason. What do you know about Rosa Parks?

Kathie: She did a lot of challenges.

Vicki: So do you think that's why you made that miscue, because Rosa Parks had a lot of challenges in her life?

Kathie: Yeah.

Conrad: On 719, she put Rosa in front of Parks, but that's a smart miscue.

Vicki: It doesn't change the meaning, and maybe it was thoughtful for Kathie to say her full name. On Kathie's retelling, she states that if it wasn't for Rosa Parks, we would still be segregated and that she is one of her American heroes. Those are all really good things to tell us, but does it tell us that you understood the piece?

Lots of head shaking.

REFLECTION

Sincere, respectful discussions became the hallmark for every group involved in RMA. It was not unusual to hear, "Oh, I do that, too!" when a student shared their tape recording, and the miscue was brought up for discussion. Nurturing behaviors and words began in careful preparation through Socratic Circles and spilled into every discussion held in the classroom, not just during RMA, the "byproduct" Vicki refers to previously.

Students began to understand the *why* behind the miscues. This is evident in statements such as, "We are used to reading longer sentences," "I think he knows another word that looks like that one," and "Maybe he was reading ahead and then had to go back and repeat." Students were no longer looking at the coded miscues in a superficial way; they understood that there was a reason for everything they were reading.

All readers miscue; therefore, proficient readers benefit from RMA just as much as struggling readers. RMA conversations focus on the kinds of things that puzzle good readers and hinder comprehension. The level of listening and support is striking. Without a doubt, the cognitive connections to reading the students made during RMA conversations provided Vicki with insight into their skills and the literacy strategies they used.

11 RMA and Developing Readers

There's no such animal!

—Jennie, a third grader

This chapter will do the following:

- Demonstrate how teachers may effectively use Retrospective Miscue Analysis (RMA) as a tool for helping developing readers
- Highlight strategies often used by the developing readers

RMA AS A TOOL FOR DEVELOPING READERS

In this chapter, we would like to share some examples of developing readers who, during RMA, became quite animated, demonstrating their excitement for the procedure and offering sophisticated comments about the reading behaviors of themselves and their classmates. In the opening quotation, Jennie is trying to explain why the miscue was not making sense in a passage saying, "There's no such animal!" These readers "found their voices" in their close-knit RMA group, no longer dominated by more articulate and successful peers in other group settings. Their behaviors transferred to other classroom discussions and activities as well.

Elizabeth, Phoenix, Jennie, Bastian, and Ron comprised Vicki's developing reading group. In the following dialogues during RMA, the use of RMA as a tool for understanding syntax and for building vocabulary is evident. As with the other groups, some interesting and insightful connections to life, text, and the world were made during RMA. With one exception, the students in this group were not particularly verbal in the classroom; however, during RMA the students became quite animated, demonstrating their excitement for the procedure and offering sophisticated comments about the reading behaviors presented to them.

STRATEGIES OFTEN USED BY DEVELOPING READERS

The students in the developing group, as in others, discussed everything from punctuation, to similarities in their miscues to the printed word, to talking about how their reading behaviors during RMA are like those they used each day for reading. During RMA conversations, their discussions turned lively as they used their words and hands to gesture when they had something important to say to the group. Good ideas for assisting other readers were articulated by the students and given as advice for enhancing reading. This group was quite astute at noticing that many readers miscue in exactly the same places; they held in-depth discussions about why that occurs.

Setting the Stage for "Speaking" Miscue

In the next dialogue, Phoenix, Jennie, Elizabeth, Ron, and Bastian listen to their taped readings and then discuss their miscues. They are reading about spiders and how they capture their prey. Vicki has already coded their miscues for the students to refer to during the discussion. Vicki gives each student a packet with the marked typescripts and instructs them to take out Ron's typescript. She then reviews the procedures for RMA. During this session, Vicki is trying to acquaint the readers with the various kinds of miscues and help them make decisions about why the reader miscued.

Vicki: What are we doing here today?

Ron: Talking about our miscues.

Vicki: Why are we doing that?

Jennie: So that we can discuss our miscues and why we make them.

Vicki: What kinds of miscues might we talk about?

Jennie: Substitutions and self-corrections.

Elizabeth: Smart and okay miscues.

Bastian: Self-corrections.

Vicki: Okay, let's listen to Ron read. Remember, you can stop the tape whenever you need to discuss a miscue.

Vicki starts the tape, and after a few minutes, Phoenix stops the tape player.

Phoenix: On line 510 he said *feet* instead of *five*. I think it was an okay miscue.

Vicki: Why do you think he said *feet* instead of *five*?

Jennie: It kind of changed the meaning. I think he was thinking about how far he jumped . . . like five feet. He might have just looked at the first letter and said *feet*.

Vicki: (Affirming Ron's prediction of meaning) And so he was maybe thinking about measurements?

The tape resumes, and this time Bastian stops the player, and the group discusses how readers sample and predict the meaning of text as they read.

Sampling and Predicting Text

Bastian: On line 551, he started to say *when* then he said *with*.

Phoenix: So maybe he was thinking of another word?

Vicki: Maybe he was thinking *where* or some other word that starts with *wh*. Then he corrected himself so that's a smart miscue.

Jennie: He said *bound* then corrected to *body*.

As the discussion continues, Vicki captures a teachable moment to point out the similarities in their reading behaviors.

Vicki: You know what? As we look at some of the other typescripts, some of you made the very same miscue. Why do you think that happened?

Ron: We're used to reading long sentences?

Vicki: Maybe it's related to that, but most of you read "the spider could only pull its legs towards its 'body' to stretch them out."

Phoenix: It still makes sense.

Bastian: He repeated spiders.

Vicki: Why do you think he did that?

Jennie: I think I know. He said *spiders* then paused to think about it and said *spiders* again.

Vicki: Do any of you ever repeat words when you're reading?

All: Oh yeah!

Vicki: What are you doing as readers when you go back and repeat words?

Elizabeth: Checking for meaning?

Word Construction, Comprehension, and Comparison of Meanings

Phoenix is the next reader; after a few minutes, Bastian stops the tape, and there is a rich discussion about word construction and how reading is all about comprehension and comparison of meanings.

Bastian: He said *spider's legs* then he paused a long time.

Vicki: Why do you think he paused?

Bastian: Maybe he looked above it and saw it.

Vicki: Yes, maybe he looked above it because it is just above it. And it ends in the same way so it would be easy to look above the word there and do the same thing.

Phoenix's miscue was marked in the following manner:

flow
floods
506 . . . the spider's special body fluids

Elizabeth: He said *flow* instead of *float*.

Vicki: I noticed he said *flows*, *floats*, and *floods*. The word is *fluids*. They all have something to do with water.

All: Yeah, they do.

Ron: He was all around it!

Vicki: Do you think it was a smart miscue?

Jennie: No, it was an okay miscue, but it was okay.

Vicki: Why was it okay?

Jennie: He could get the meaning enough to keep on going. Back here when he said *sinks* he was trying to sound out *sinking*.

Elizabeth: On line 506, he said *floods*, then *flows* for *fluids*. He went all around the word but didn't get it.

At this point, Vicki leaves the group to greet a classroom visitor. The video recorder is still going, and the next conversation takes place without the teacher. When Elizabeth continues the RMA conversation as Vicki exits the group, we see a rich example of how readers can take ownership of the RMA discussion.

Elizabeth: On line 508, he said *explode* for *expands*. It changes the meaning.

Phoenix read the two lines like this:

507 Did you ever pour water into a balloon and see it
explode
508 expand. The jumping spider's legs stretch the same way. But . . .

Elizabeth: (She is continuing the conversation about the *explode* miscue.) If you fill a balloon up with too much air, it explodes.

Jennie: I think it's an okay miscue. He is using clues from what he knows about balloons.

Vicki returns to the group and without asking for a summary of the conversation that occurred in her absence, re-explores the same miscue they just discussed. She recalls the irony of situation, remembering her explanation was not as thoughtful as those offered by Elizabeth and Jennie. We later discussed this. So many times, teachers new to RMA take the lead too much, and when the conversations are not videotaped or recorded, some of the critical inquiry skills that readers like Elizabeth and Jennie exhibit are lost. Another teacher new to RMA once dubbed these "teaching miscues."

Exploring Language Conventions

The next miscue is an interpretation of language conventions (hyphenation) already explored by the more proficient reading group in Chapter 11. The readers explicate this language convention and why it is so difficult for them to deal with when reading.

Ron: He says *happens* then *pens* then repeats pens on lines 508 and 509.

Vicki: It is a hyphenated word so maybe that's why Phoenix did that?

Elizabeth: Hyphenated words make me stop sometimes.

Jennie: They sort of make you sound out the word, and it doesn't always come out right.

Vicki: You mean it doesn't sound like language?

Sounds of Meaning

The discussion then extends from hyphenation to a related reading strategy. Their conversation about the need for text to "sound like language" comes full circle.

Jennie: On line 511, he says *could* instead of *would*. It didn't change the meaning, but he corrected himself anyway.

Vicki: What do you hear Phoenix doing a lot when reading aloud?

Ron: He sounds out the word partly, and it might not be quite the right word, but he then self-corrects.

(Elizabeth verbally sounds out *imagine* trying out Phoenix's strategy.)

Elizabeth: *Im . . . ma . . . gine*. I do that, too!

Jennie: In one book I was reading, the word I couldn't get was *repulsive*, and I had to sound it out three times!

Once again, Vicki seizes a teachable moment to move the readers from the use of one strategy to suggest another.

Looking at Words in Context

As a part of classroom literacy instruction, Vicki emphasized the use of context words for greater comprehension and fluency, but the developing readers still relied heavily on "sounding out" as a primary strategy. However, in the following analysis, the use of context clues becomes authentic for the readers through the text.

Vicki: Do you ever use the words around the word to help you? Look at lines 508 and 509. If you didn't know what *launching* meant, what are some context clues to help you figure it out?

> The jumping spider's legs stretch the same way. But it happens very fast, launching the spider into the air.

All: Into the air!

Navigating Nonfiction Text

Elizabeth is the next reader. They listen to her entire tape then discuss her miscues. For many struggling readers, nonfiction text presents greater challenges because the predictability of narrative story is missing. Notice how the miscues of the readers and their rationale behind them are similar.

Vicki: Have you ever noticed that when you're reading nonfiction text, the sentences are shorter to help you understand better?

All: Yeah.

Vicki: Would you read this text differently from fiction text?

Elizabeth: Definitely!

Jennie: You'd read this slower and may have to reread more to understand.

Abigail: You said *waters* not *fluids.*

Jennie: I think she kept on going with the sentence and said *water* since we have water in our body.

Elizabeth: I thought *water* meant the same as *fluids.*

Good ideas for assisting other readers are articulated by the students and given as advice for enhancing reading during Socratic Circle intervals. Teachers may capture and use comments and discussions expressed during Socratic Circles intervals and RMA conversations to enhance instruction in other subject areas where reading is a critical component such as social studies and science. For example, recorded student comments about how readers made comparisons and connections to life or other text may be used to introduce concepts associated with other aspects of the curriculum. In addition, these comments may assist in demonstrating how comparisons and connections to life or other texts may occur across subject areas.

REFLECTION

RMA is an organic process grounded in specific strategies but flexible enough to accommodate the conversations of all types of readers that spring up in the process. During RMA conversations, discussions become lively as readers use their words and hands to gesture when they have something important to say to the group. RMA draws out the developing reader through the process of inquiry and problem solving as miscues become puzzles to solve as well as frameworks for interesting, engaging classroom conversation.

(Continued)

(Continued)

Teachers who use RMA involve readers in discussions about everything from punctuation, to similarities in words that were miscued compared to the print, to talking about how their reading behaviors during RMA are like those they use each day for all kinds of learning. RMA encouraged Vicki's developing readers to form an appreciation for reading by exploring their own reading processes while Socratic Circles affirmed these readers with motivating and insightful comments from classmates. For example Autumn and Ron, especially, always noted when peers remembered to pay attention to text features like captions or headings or pointed them out themselves. While difficult to measure gains in enthusiasm and motivation on standardized tests, it was evident to Vicki that her developing readers' abilities to recall and problem solve their way through text improved significantly, and at least in Jennie's case, as the reader will find in Chapter 13, those newly discovered reading strategies stayed with her after moving to another grade level.

12 RMA and Striving Readers

Because I'm looking at the other sentence so I can make sure I get it right.

—Scott, a third grader

> This chapter will do the following:
>
> - Demonstrate strategies that assist striving readers who have difficulty making multiple connections to text
> - Explore how Retrospective Miscue Analysis (RMA) motivates striving readers to critically inquire into the reading process
> - Show how well striving readers advised and supported one another during RMA
> - Explain the need for greater teacher participation in RMA with striving readers

MAKING MULTIPLE CONNECTIONS TO TEXT

The readers profiled in this chapter represent those who struggled more with reading than the other two groups. The next reading example is a passage about prairie dog behaviors and habitat from *Prairie Dog's Burrow* (Kline, 2002). They are listening to David's tape.

```
             dogs
101    Prairie Dog works hard.
                       into
102    She stomps dirt onto the
       mud
103    mound. One prairie dog
```

Their comments are thoughtful and take on a problem solving tone. They discuss reading strategies, "okay" miscues, and even how readers take information from one part of the text to combine with another resulting in what is a reasonable miscue. In this group of striving readers, the students made many important discoveries about their reading.

Water Plus Dirt Equals Mud

In the following conversation, Molly and Abigail focused on how David pronounced *mud* for *mound*. There is an allusion to water and dirt in the text, and they thoughtfully suggest this orientation prompted the miscue.

Molly: He said *pred* for *predators* at first.

David: I didn't know the word at the beginning.

Molly: Sounding out helps you read.

Molly: He said *mud* for *mound*. He didn't really see the *o*.

David: I agree with Molly.

(The group agrees it was an okay miscue.)

Abigail: Water plus dirt equals mud. . . .

Molly: He said *flocks* instead of *falcons*. That's an okay miscue.

David: I didn't see *a*; I thought *o*.

Abigail: Maybe the words got jumbled up.

In this dialogue, it is evident how RMA empowers the reader to discuss miscues of language in a safe, productive forum. Abigail points out the connection, "Well, water plus dirt equals mud," thus giving everyone in the group and class an insightful glimpse into how the mind sometimes works as we read. When readers are shown how to use their own voices and ideas during RMA conversations, teachers will discover that the less confident readers emerge with confidence and conviction.

CRITICAL INQUIRY INTO THE READING PROCESS

In the following discussion, the striving readers are talking about struggling to make sense of text and looking for ways to become self-reliant readers.

Jackson: I'm really not a good "rememberer."

Molly: Me either. I get distracted, and it's hard then because, like you get all these words in your mind, and you have to go through them.

Abigail: You get things jumbled in your head.

Vicki: What do you do to get things unjumbled, to help you remember clearly what you read?

Molly: I try to think very hard.

Abigail: I tried reviewing the book. My brother asks me questions.

Jackson: Yes, my mom does too.

Vicki: Do you ever think aloud to yourself? Just thinking aloud helps.

David: I try it at home sometimes.

Speaking in Miscue

The striving or lower ability readers quickly became proficient at "speaking in miscue," much like the developing and proficient readers. Participating in Socratic Circles later ensured that all the readers in Vicki's classroom were comfortable with and understood the differences between the miscues and how they were marked on pieces of text. In the next dialogue, Vicki is teaching the readers to "speak in miscue" by helping them understand the difference between a "smart" and an "okay" miscue.

Molly: On line 911, he forgot the word *again*, and then after fences, he said *and* instead of *or*.

Vicki: Let's read that the way he read it: "But when she ran, she crashed into trees, fences, and fell or hurt herself." Do you think that's an okay miscue or a smart miscue?

Molly: It's an okay miscue; no, it's a smart miscue. Because it doesn't really affect the meaning.

Abigail: I think I would rather read it the way that David read it.

David: I think I would have put a comma there rather instead of *and*.

ADVISING AND SUPPORTING ONE ANOTHER

There were a number of other strategies established through RMA conversations, particularly evident among the striving or struggling readers.

We characterize those as strategies that led to a strong literacy community within the classroom with mutual respect and understanding of each member as a literate person. A few examples follow:

The striving readers sometimes got stuck on the mechanics of reading. We know that a reader's eyes travel all over the page while engaged in the reading process—sometimes to look back and confirm, sometimes to look ahead to predict, and sometimes to look at any illustrations that would assist in confirming or predicting. And a reader's eyes do not always stay on the lines they are intending to read. In the following dialogue, the RMA conversation about miscues turns to advice giving about how David can help himself when his eyes do not stay on the line he is reading:

Scott: On line 707, he said *mother* instead of *father*.

Vicki: Except, look! What did he do?

Scott: He went back and corrected.

Vicki: He corrected himself. Why would he read *mother* instead of *father*?

Abigail: Because he was probably thinking about his mother. Or maybe on 906, he probably read that line, and that line was in his head.

Vicki: That's exactly what I think happened. Do you think it's possible that his eye went to the line above, and he just read mother? There are also quite a lot of similarities in the way those two words look. They're spelled nearly the same, aren't they? And Abigail, I think you're absolutely right. Does that ever happen to you where your eyes flip to the line above or below what you're reading?

David: Yes, because I am kind of like . . . well it's kind of . . . I just popped my brain up to mother. I said *mother* and then popped it back down to *father*.

Molly: What I do at home is just, I'll put the bookmark right here and keep going down and down.

Vicki: Does it help you, Molly, if you can see the line above and below, or do you really need to isolate the line you are reading?

Molly: The line I'm reading because if I don't, I'll skip to the other line, and then it doesn't make sense.

Vicki: Do any of you need to see the line above or below? I'm kind of one of those people. I need to see the words around so it makes sense.

Scott: At my babysitter's, she has little strips of paper from her paper shredder that I use.

Vicki: Those are really skinny so that you can still see the lines above and below. That's a really good idea, Scott!

In another RMA session, the students are discussing text about Helen Keller. Vicki and the students in the group are offering support to Scott.

Vicki: I had an observation about Scott's reading overall. I noticed that Scott is a very careful reader. He reads slowly and very carefully.

Abigail: That's probably why he doesn't have very many miscues.

Vicki: Good observation, Abigail, and I think he understands what he reads.

Vicki: I think that sometimes you (Scott) don't see yourself as a good reader. But I think you are a very good reader. What about the rest of you?

All three give Scott a thumbs up.

The group continues with a very long discussion about fevers. Abigail is puzzled about why the text doesn't tell them what kind of fever Helen has and desires clarification on what caused Helen to be blind and deaf. The students are very animated holding their hands to their foreheads and making connections to when they have been ill or have brothers and sisters who have been ill with very high fevers, thus sharing common experiences as a group.

TEACHER PARTICIPATION

Note that in each of the dialogues of this chapter, Vicki is "heard" much more than she was in other groups. We feel this is due to the fact that sometimes struggling (striving) readers need greater scaffolding and assistance as they develop their understanding of themselves as readers. In following RMA session with the striving readers, there is a long discussion about Scott's miscues and retelling. Scott is one of the quietest students in the classroom and did not participate as much as his peers in RMA discussions. He had a long history of disliking school, especially any tasks requiring reading. For this group, Vicki often had to facilitate the discussions to keep them going. However, his RMA group shows compassion and respect for Scott's reading ability as they help him understand reasons for his miscues and assist each other in making connections to life experiences and other text:

Abigail: On line 909, that's a very long pause.

Vicki: Why do you think he did that?

Abigail: He was probably thinking.

Vicki: Scott, do you know why you make pauses when you read?

Scott: Because I'm looking at the other sentence so I can make sure I get it right.

Vicki: So you're reading ahead?

Scott shakes his head affirming that he is reading ahead.

Vicki: What do you think (speaking to Scott)?

Scott: Pretty good.

Vicki: You have an excellent retelling. Jackson is right; the only detail that you left out is that she is blind and deaf. You say that she became very ill, and the doctor didn't know what to do because she was too ill. That isn't in the text, but you figured it out because you said she was always running into things.

Monitoring teacher talk is critical during RMA, but the above transcription provides an example of a student actually needing extra support from the teacher. While Scott was often silent during RMA conversations as well as other classroom contexts, he did find his voice when the RMA sessions revolved around his audiotape. However, it still requires skillful facilitation from Vicki to help him understand the reasoning behind his miscues.

REFLECTION

The process of RMA empowers even the lowest ability groups to critically and deeply think about text, rethink their miscues, and make significant connections to the text. The RMA group members knew they were becoming better readers and why. Molly tells Vicki that she was able to listen to other people read the same passage she had and to see multiple ways of constructing text and meaning. This is a significant difference in this approach to teaching reading than say, round robin reading, or even taking turns reading in small groups. The instructional quality is heightened because readers are invited to inquire, to dig deep, and to think about their miscues as windows into the reading processes of each one of them. As Molly points out, she did not view RMA as just another instructional strategy like guided reading or others. The third graders were beginning to isolate and examine their strengths as readers and to choose reading strategies that worked the best for them as individual readers and learners.

Perhaps more than in any other group, the striving readers learned how to analyze the reading process in authentic learning contexts in which student opinions mattered. The constructive feedback they received from their peers led to the establishment of classroom community that might have not been possible using a more prescriptive approach to teaching reading. The children were empowered to use their voices to own the reading process and to respect and include every reader's assessment of the reading and learning process.

13 Concluding Thoughts and Follow-Up Interviews

You could ask yourself some different questions.

—Phoenix, a third grader

This chapter will do the following:

- Summarize the benefits of Retrospective Miscue Analysis (RMA) to students, teachers, and parents
- Share two follow-up interviews one year after RMA

RMA BENEFITS

In our work with readers, we have noted several benefits from RMA for both students and teachers. The most important benefit in RMA is that it changes how students, teachers, and sometimes parents view the reading process. When readers are encouraged to talk about their miscues rather than their "mistakes," they look at reading differently. The motivation level goes up instantly as readers realize that reading is not just pronouncing words correctly; it is creating and building meaning by integrating the author's text with their own background knowledge and experiences. They also begin to understand the interdisciplinary nature of the reading program when they are encouraged to make connections to text based on other readings and experiences. As we stated earlier in the introduction to the book, after conducting a miscue analysis, teachers will never listen to a child read in the same way again.

Students

Children often view reading as a single subject. Allison, a third grader, told Rita that reading was her most dreaded subject, but Rita knew from observation that she was a voracious reader. After probing a bit, Rita learned that Allison loved to read books but did not make the connection between learning about reading in the classroom to the act of reading. RMA focuses directly on the act of reading not reading as a single subject of instruction. Readers gain greater control of all kinds of texts by problem solving their way through the text as they listen to and interpret their use of reading strategies. Our definition of *text* in this book extends beyond the printed page, as we have seen the inquiry and problem solving strategies learned in RMA and used by students to conduct research across content areas and even to help them problem solve on standardized tests.

Another benefit of RMA conversations is that readers of all abilities learn about various strategies from one another like Phoenix in the opening quotation who suggested self-questioning as a way of monitoring for meaning. Another example comes from Nathan, a fourth grader from a study Rita conducted a few years ago, who sometimes read a word incorrectly the first time but figured it out later as he continued to read. During an RMA session in which two boys of varying reading levels were paired, he pointed out to his friend Justin who was struggling with the word *treacherous* that if he kept on reading, he would figure out the word from the "other words around it." Nathan was considered a low-level reader, and Justin was making high grades in reading (Moore & Gilles, 2005). Phoenix's quotation at the beginning of this chapter is also a good example of how readers in RMA groups begin to share the reading strategies they use.

Classroom dynamics supported through RMA "talk" demonstrate to children that all learners have something to offer. When Rita visited Vicki's classroom, she observed that during RMA conversations, the children seemed oblivious to ability levels; they were most intent on performing their tasks as members of the RMA group or the outer Socratic Circle. It was hard to believe that this classroom represented an unusual number of learning and behavioral disabilities because the behaviors of the children were focused on the important tasks of reading and connecting their talk about reading to their lives and experiences as learners. The culture and community of the classroom relied on mutual respect and interest in what other readers had to say about their interpretations of text or the reading strategies they were using rather than on who was a better reader or who was a more successful learner.

In our combined experiences with RMA and Socratic Circles, we have never encountered unwilling or disrespectful students. RMA is an instructional approach to developing a democratic learning community, and instead of making fun of a struggling peer, the process promotes students who support one another by speaking about similar miscues they also make while reading. Classroom teachers who feel students might not honor the privacy of a peer should establish norms for RMA and/or Socratic Circles before beginning. Speaking about Socratic Circles, Copeland (2005) acknowledges teachers possibly fear releasing control to students but also notes he is "continually amazed at how mature students can act when given the opportunity to do so" (p. 73).

Teachers

Teachers who listen to children verbally explore the meaning behind their miscues and their retelling of text may never teach in the same way again (Moore & Gilles, 2005). As well, teachers who learn to implement RMA into reading instruction gain greater insights into the reading process by examining patterns emerging from both the miscues and retellings, thus becoming much better at reflection and diagnosis of reading strengths and weaknesses (Worsnop, 1996). For example, Autumn, a student in Vicki's class, was able to recall important conclusions, but her ideas were not recalled in logical order. That information helped Vicki choose strategies and activities that strengthened Autumn's ability to put ideas in order.

In another classroom incident, one of Rita's college students was conducting a retelling. The second grader was obviously confused by the terms *setting* and *character*. The college student stopped the retelling and asked the child, "What is a character?" The child confidently responded, "It's where the story happens." Knowing the child thought *character* meant *setting* was quite helpful to the child's classroom teacher!

RMA is a different kind of assessment and evaluation tool that defines children as readers, not as test scores. Vicki, now a literacy coach for three elementary schools in Kansas, often talks about her observations of how we tend to "see" our students through test scores rather than "knowing" our students as readers. When asked about a student's reading success or lack of it, teachers may talk about test performance or percentile ranking in the class. Sadly, data-driven "talk" defined only around standardized test scores has led to an environment where teachers are not encouraged to discuss what books, authors, or genres their students might be interested in reading.

The work within RMA gives us insight into readers like no other process we, as teachers, have engaged in previously. Because students are articulating what happens when they read, we see them in a whole new light—a critical piece often missing from our view of students as readers. Students often make connections to other texts they are reading or have read in the RMA process, which helps teachers know the kinds of texts students are interested in reading. Teachers listening to RMA conversations about miscues or retellings will hear patterns of reading behavior that lead to other kinds of teaching (Goodman, 2003), extending into many aspects of the curriculum and school day.

In the midst of current state and federal demands to have scientifically based reading curricula, there is a wealth of research supporting RMA, although in the flurry of Reading First initiatives, much of this research has been set aside. Building instruction on published program materials rather than on well-researched and documented knowledge about how children learn to read simply did not work according to the latest report from the Institute of Education Sciences. The study of the 17 school districts of the sample noted that while instructional time using materials from federally approved scientifically based reading instruction in phonemic awareness, phonics, vocabulary, fluency, and comprehension increased, the impact on reading comprehension measured by standardized test scores was not significant (USDE, 2008). The fact that Reading First policies and procedures failed to significantly improve reading comprehension in Grades 1–3 indicates that teachers need the flexibility and resources to provide instruction that meets the needs of all readers (IRA, 2008) and values the role of the reader in the reading process.

Parents

Most recently, we have encouraged parents to utilize some of the techniques of RMA at home as they talk about vocabulary from shared readings as well as retellings. RMA participants (teachers, students, or parents) assume an active, empowered role in the reading process and begin to think of reading as a process or even a tool for learning. When parents understand that they do not have to teach reading in a didactic manner, rather that children learn as much or more from talk about reading and miscues in reading, then reading at home becomes a natural part of home culture, rather than another task to do on busy week nights.

One parent said to a teacher who used RMA in the classroom and encouraged parents to do so as well, "We put words on the fridge now that we want to talk about instead of looking them up in the dictionary. Conversations like these have changed attitudes toward reading at our house."

RMA provides in-depth information to share with parents during face-to-face conferences or meetings about student progress. A marked miscue sheet and transcribed retelling simply explained to parents provides tangible evidence of what we previously have only been able to discuss using words or scores. That information coupled with the critical dialogue the teacher has participated in with the student gives insight into a child's progress we have lacked in the past.

Once Vicki presented this kind of information to parents, there were many, like the parent of a student Vicki tutored using RMA, who said, "Yes, now that you have shown me and explained this to me, I have seen her do that at home too. Now, we can talk about it during reading time at home." Currently a literacy coach, Vicki was recently asked to participate in the classroom teacher's parent-teacher conference of this same student. After the parents left, the classroom teacher was in awe of the information that Vicki had gleaned from conducting a few RMA sessions with this student. She told Vicki afterward, "You had so much information about [the student] to tell her parents, and I learned so much about her reading strengths and weaknesses than I had from what I am currently doing in the classroom during reading." This incident helped the teacher rethink her approach to classroom reading instruction as well as how she might better connect with parents.

JAIMIE, ONE YEAR LATER

An abbreviated follow-up discussion one year later with Jaimie, one of the students in the "average reader" group, follows as she voices how RMA changed her thinking about herself as a reader and a learner and her feelings about books. This emphasizes the value of RMA in supporting and developing lifelong readers. From the beginning of their discussion, Jaimie is able to tell Vicki how RMA helped her, and although she is not as articulate about exactly what she means, the conversation is important. When asked what she remembered about RMA, Jaimie said, "It always ended up helping me. It helped me understand lots of things—ways to say words." In further discussion prompted by Vicki, Jaimie clarified that RMA assisted her getting "at" words beyond simple sounding out strategies. She was able to use context clues to figure out unknown words or words she had little prior experience while reading but had heard used in conversations.

Jaimie also recognized that RMA helped her become metacognitive about her reading; she was not someone who was just reading words on a page. When asked about listening to the audiotapes of herself reading within the group setting and how those experiences impacted her as a reader, she stated, "I thought a lot of times I didn't do very well on tests." Jaimie is referring to the computerized tests offered by Accelerated Reader (AR), a schoolwide reading initiative to which Vicki struggled to stay faithful when seeing the detrimental effect that failing scores had on her students' self-concepts as readers. When the emphasis on AR was removed or reduced, and the emphasis was placed on guided reading structures, specifically RMA and Socratic Circles, students began to believe in themselves as readers. Jaimie followed her first sentence with, "I thought I got better at reading." Taking away the emphasis on the literal comprehension assessment offered by AR and becoming focused instead on the reading process was meaningful to Jaimie and changed her beliefs in herself as a reader.

This new insight for Jaimie is further illustrated when she is asked to talk about what parts of RMA have helped her with reading since her third-grade year. She says, "I have done tapes on my own. I did [read] harder books—it helped me with my STAR report, and I was able to read five-point books."

Vicki believes that while Jaimie is still using the Accelerated Reader program and taking the STAR testing component offered by Reading Renaissance to place students in a range of reading levels, she has also learned to help herself by tape recording herself reading and then listening to it. Here we can see that Jaimie clearly understood and valued listening to herself read, applying what she had learned in RMA. It was important to Jaimie to be able to read books that could earn her points as an incentive, and she found a way to do that on her own. She realizes that RMA helped her to move away from safe, short books to longer, more challenging material. She stated, "Bigger books interest me more now."

In their discussion, Jaimie acknowledged to Vicki that she still has difficulty reading sometimes. She said that "hard, big, long words" still give her trouble as do "too many small words on a page." She expands on this by saying, "Sometimes I get lost on a page and have to read over and over," but she also stated that RMA helped her to remember to move on when she gets stuck on the same line. Perhaps the most poignant statement Jaimie made during their discussion was one showing that she is now armed with new strategies and "in charge" of her reading: "I try to fix it on my own now." Empowering readers to know the benefits of becoming independent readers is critical to learning success. In RMA, no one but the reader writes the script for reading instruction, and the outcomes are powerful.

JENNA, ONE YEAR LATER

Vicki saw Jenna one year later too. She interviewed Jenna to determine her perception of how effective the RMA process had been in helping her with her reading skills and how she sees herself as a reader. Jenna was less likely to elaborate on her thoughts than Jaimie, but one can still see how she used the RMA process to think about reading. She speaks about the "grown up" nature of RMA when she says that it surprised her that "we were in groups by ourselves" and that "we had to tape record." It is the first time that Vicki realized that the students did not see RMA as an instructional process just like any other in her classroom (such as guided reading groups). Instead, Jenna viewed RMA as quite different and valued the independent nature of the work. It is important to note that the students were never by themselves, but it is now that Vicki realizes she was truly seen as a facilitator rather than a teacher by the children in the groups.

Jenna noticed what she does as a reader by listening to herself on the audiotapes. This surfaced in the discussion with Vicki when she says, "I repeated a lot. I struggled on some of the words. I didn't stop at periods and commas." Everything that Jenna stated is true, but she had no insight into her reading behaviors before engagement in RMA. She is able to say how RMA has assisted her with her reading since: "Sometimes I read to my dad," clarifying for Vicki that it is still important for her to "hear" herself reading aloud to someone else, serving to assist her in improving her skills. She stated, "I stop on periods and commas now"—a skill she is proud of improving. However, Jenna knows there is still work ahead when she says, "I struggle on words still sometime" and notes that she still has trouble with word endings.

Jenna gained some strategies through the RMA process as well. When asked what she does now when she is stuck, she said, "I go back and reread the sentence. I break it down. If I don't know the word, I'll look it up in the dictionary." All of these are strategies Jenna carried with her beyond third grade to assist her in becoming a successful reader. During the interview, she confirmed the benefit of learning that other students miscue, just as she does, when she stated, "You got to listen to other people read it," in response to Vicki's question of how RMA helped Jenna become a better reader.

REFLECTION

All readers are invited to participate in RMA conversations, either as listeners or as speakers. The RMA process serves as a framework for making significant connections to other texts, to themselves, and to the world beyond the classroom. The process is easily explained to parents who can encourage the same critical literacy thinking processes at home and beyond. RMA is a flexible approach to teaching reading that thoughtfully reveals the reading process. It is particularly helpful to struggling readers who need to understand that reading is a process of making meaning not merely an exercise in decoding words. They must learn to trust their own understanding of how language works—what sounds right, what does not, and why. While our research continues as we follow readers who have participated in RMA, children like Jenna and Jaimie have benefited.

Resources

Resource A

A Summary of the Research

RMA: A SCIENTIFICALLY RESEARCHED APPROACH TO TEACHING READING

Having a sound research base from which to teach has always been necessary for quality instruction. In today's climate of accountability, it is more important than ever to be able to cite the research and theory behind our practice. For that reason, we include a short summary of the research supporting RMA.

Retrospective miscue analysis is grounded in extensive reading miscue analysis research that began with the work of Ken Goodman (1968, 1969) and continued through his ongoing research (Goodman, 1996b) and that of others (see Alan & Watson, 1977; Bloome & Dail, 1997; Y. Goodman, Watson, & Burke, 1987, 2005; Goodman, 1995; Martens, 1998; and Watson, 1978, 1996a, 1996b). RMA is rooted in linguistic research rather than reductionist or skills-based research, in which decoding text correctly and in sequence is the primary focus of reading instruction (K. Goodman, 1994). Linguistic researchers "consider reading as an active, receptive language process and readers as users of language" (Bloome & Dail, 1997; Goodman, 1994, 1996a, 1996b).

Research into the analysis of oral reading miscues demonstrates that "miscues are unexpected responses cued by the reader's knowledge of that language and concepts of the world . . . when expected and unexpected responses match, we get few insights into this process. When they do not match and a miscue results, teachers as researchers have a 'window' on the reading process" (Goodman, 1973, p. 5). For the purpose of informing instructional practice, the teacher may look for patterns in these mismatches to document what readers know about the pragmatic and semantic (meaning), syntactic (grammar), and graphophonic (letter and/or sound association) language cueing systems (Goodman, 1996b; Weaver, 1980, 1994), and how they use that knowledge to make sense of text. More recently, educators like Wilde (2000) and Davenport (2002) have published versions of miscue analysis to fit into reading workshop or as

---

SOURCE: Adapted from Moore & Gilles, 2005, with permission.

data for reading conferences with the intent of building on student strengths and helping teachers better understand students as readers. RMA is different only in that it directly involves the reader in making decisions about and investigating the reader's own miscues. The information the teacher learns about the reader comes from the miscue analysis and the RMA discussions. Teachers who are interested in more information about miscue analysis may wish to consult *Reading Miscue Inventory* (Goodman, Watson, & Burke, 1987), *Reading Miscue Inventory: From Evaluation to Instruction for All Readers* (Goodman, Watson, & Burke, 2005), *Miscue Analysis Made Easy* (Wilde, 2000), or *Miscues Not Mistakes* (Davenport, 2002).

RMA is strongly linked to the research in socio-psycholinguistics, which reveals intricate connections between the social, cognitive, and linguistic aspects of reading and language development (Goodman, 1973; Weaver, 1980, 1994). During RMA conversations, readers are invited to make social, personal, and cognitive connections to text to better understand the reading and language process. Once they understand what really happens as they read, they are empowered to make decisions about their own interpretations of meaning. Consider this metaphor: how do you learn to swim if you have no knowledge of what it means to swim? Reading works the same way. One of the best ways to help children understand the reading process is to engage them in discussion about their reading miscues and retellings, thus providing them with evidence of the language systems at work (Moore & Gilles, 2005).

Extensive miscue analysis and RMA research demonstrates that reading is not simply a process of decoding, although decoding is integral to the process. The research clearly demonstrates to teachers and students what readers *do* when they read; they take their background knowledge and apply it to all they know about language as they predict and confirm the meaning of the text. Goodman (1973) suggests they create parallel texts to the author's texts. Davenport (2002) explains,

> While a reader is trying to understand what the author is saying, she or he is building her or his own meaning, which will always vary slightly from the author's intended meaning. This personally constructed text governs what the reader perceives and the syntax that is assigned to what is read. As the reader is constructing both the structure and meaning of the text, sometimes the text in the reader's head must be reconstructed to maintain meaning. (p. 13)

Some readers need more help than others in figuring out the reading process. RMA gives readers the opportunity to do so as they examine patterns in their miscues such as substitutions, omissions, insertions, or placeholders. These patterns provide evidence that they are using their knowledge of language to create meaning from text.

Retrospective miscue analysis draws on a variety of research: the value of classroom talk (Barnes, 1975, 1992; Barnes, Britton, & Rosen, 1969; Barnes, Britton, & Torbe, 1990; Pierce & Gilles, 1993; Wells, 1986; Wells & Chang-Wells, 1992); social interaction (K. Goodman, 1996b; Vygotsky, 1978); and learner empowerment issues (Christian & Bloome, 2004; Gore, 1993). Also informing RMA is Rosenblatt's work (1978), exploring how readers transact with text not as a one-way exchange between author and reader but as a two-way transaction in which the reader actively engages in creating meaning from text. RMA is strongly linked to research in socio-psycholinguistics, which reveals intricate connections between the social, cognitive, and linguistic aspect of reading and language development (Lindfors, 1991; Smith, 1994; Weaver, 1994).

The constructivist nature of RMA is grounded in the work of Vygotsky (1978), especially related is articulating one's thoughts while constructing meaning. The learner is participating in deconstructing knowledge while also reconstructing knowledge that is closely tied to Vygotsky's theories of socially interactive learning and the notion that these kinds of interactions eventually lead the reader to rely less on knowledgeable others—sometimes called a "gradual release of responsibility" (Pearson & Gallagher, 1983).

The use of RMA by teachers originated from a process called reader-selected miscues (RSM), developed by Dorothy Watson to spark classroom discussions about reading among junior high students (Watson, 1978; Watson & Hoge, 1996). In RSM, readers select words that troubled them during silent reading and then discuss those miscues with a teacher or a small group. Later, Worsnop (1980) worked with struggling adolescents readers (see also Watson, 1978; Watson & Hoge, 1996), and Marek (1987) conducted her dissertation research with a troubled adult reader named Gina. Marek's research was then used as the foundation for developing a study on the effectiveness of using RMA with seventh graders (Goodman & Flurkey, 1996). In each of these studies, struggling readers gained greater understanding of the reading process and became more confident, fluent readers. Improvement in reading grades and increased interest in leisure reading were also noted.

RMA is an approach to reading assessment and instruction originally published by Y. Goodman and Marek (1996) as a reading strategy for middle school and older readers. Later, RMA was reflected in the work of many researchers who conducted studies with teachers and particularly puzzling, struggling readers (Goodman & Marek, 1996; Martens, 1998;

Moore & Aspegren, 2001; Moore & Brantingham, 2003). In each of these studies, word recognition and comprehension scores improved dramatically, and fluency improvement followed. In addition, teachers using RMA developed a much better understanding of what readers *do* when they read as they listened carefully to (1) graphophonic patterns in oral reading, (2) syntactic patterns in oral reading, and (3) semantic patterns both in oral reading and in retelling of text.

Research in RMA has grown to include readers in the elementary grades. Through the work of researchers such as Gilles & Dickenson (2000), Martens (1998), and Moore & Brantingham (2003), we are beginning to understand how RMA works with developing and struggling readers. In her dissertation work, Folger (2001) looked at text construction with readers participating in RMA. She found that readers used their knowledge of language at word, sentence, and story levels to make connections to their own experiences and in visualizing and constructing parallel texts. Her results are consistent with what researchers using RMA with older readers have asserted: students moved away from relying solely on phonetic decoding; they became more metacognitive about their reading process, and they showed an increase in strategy use. McDonald (2008) sought to move away from the behaviorist models often used with students enrolled in special education classrooms, toward a constructivist model of learning often defined in the work of Piaget (Duckworth, 2006). McDonald (2008) found that the students in her classroom were capable of engagement in RMA, improved their metacognitive skills related to reading, and produced changes in their views about themselves as readers as well as their perspective of the reading process.

Other studies continue to build on what the reader, regardless of age, brings to the reading event as they help students focus more on reading strengths rather than weaknesses. Even the youngest readers are cognizant of their reading abilities and provide us with an insight into what they do well in reading and where they lack skills (Davenport, Lauritzen, & Smith, 2002). Building on our knowledge about early readers, a recent study by Pahls-Weiss (2004) conducted in an early childhood placement examined the effects of using RMA with first-grade students. Pahls-Weiss (2004) too found that first-grade students who participated in RMA began to take a more analytical approach to reading, increased their use of the syntactic and semantic cueing systems, and decreased repetitions—indicating more efficient reading. This growing body of research suggests that regardless of age, RMA helps readers become more efficient and effective readers.

RMA opens the door to well-rounded literacy instruction that spans the curriculum. According to Lauritzen (2009), the research shows that single-focused instruction does not lead to the development of literacy in children. In fact, the National Early Literacy Panel (NELP) found that when instruction included "high quality teacher-student interaction" then variables of literacy achievement were positively impacted (Lauritzen, 2009, p. 11). Another finding was that the most effective instructional interventions occurred in small groups of students with a well-prepared teacher. By participating in discussions with students about the skills they bring to the table during any literacy task, we honor those readers' strengths and what they know about reading. Wilson (2005) summarizes, "many teachers remind struggling readers of their weaknesses, often taking for granted that students know their strengths" (p. 29).

Grouping for learning is a common practice in the classroom, but the use of collaborative learning strategies within groups defines RMA and CRMA. Collaborative learning in a classroom is a process, something constructed rather than an isolated incident occurring to complete a task or project (Johnston, 2004) and encompasses individuals discussing and generating ideas and "eliciting thinking that surpasses individual effort" (Costa, 2008, p. 116). Collaborative learning is akin to what Watson (1996) describes as a "community of learners" as opposed to a "collection of people" where the "chemistry stems from a sense of community created by all the learners who share not only space and time but themselves as scholars and friends" (p. 269).

In addition, miscue analysis and aspects of RMA are more and more present in the research associated with English Language Learners (ELL). The work of Hudelson (1984), Freeman and Freeman (2006), and Whitmore and Crowell (1994) provide excellent resources for teachers who may not speak the first languages of all their students but who want all of the readers' voices to be heard. Research into how miscue analysis and RMA works with ELL children of all ages is beginning to become more prominent. It is predicated on the idea that the linguistic systems function much the same in any language (Goodman, 1996b). The work of Hudelson (1984), Freeman and Freeman (2006), and Whitmore and Crowell (1994) in miscue and RMA with ELLs provide excellent resources for teachers.

Goodman (2007) reminds us that one of the most critical pieces of information known about ELLs is they may be able to read silently in English then discuss or retell in their L1 with a classmate who speaks the same L1. Reading in English and retelling in the L1 provides a bridge between reading and speaking the second language (Brisk & Harrington, 2007; Goodman, 2007). In addition, the examination of miscues by ELLs allow teachers to understand how much English language learning is taking place such as knowing how to use determiners such as "a" or "the" interchangeably (Goodman, 2007).

And finally, eye movement research by Cattell (1886) from the late 1800s showed that readers do not look at every word while reading. Follow-up research by Delabarre (1898) was conducted with an instrument he developed for eye movement tracking. While eye movement research has shown for years that readers' eyes move faster than their oral reading, the technology that accompanies current eye-movement research allows us to see the reader's movements from the beginning to the end of the sentence, to an illustration, or even to pick up a word a few lines down to insert in the text the voice has marked. The more recent research of Peter Duckett (2003) shows that beginning readers sample print and illustrations in a continuous effort to predict and confirm meaning. Devices used in the research that combine the voice and eye movement of the reader present teachers with some rich scenarios for miscue analysis and would be fascinating to use with readers during RMA conversations (Paulson & Freeman, 2003). In addition, Goodman, Watson, and Burke (2005) include a chapter on eye movements and the relationship to understanding reading in their updated version of the *Reading Miscue Inventory.*

As the reader will notice, many of the allusions in RMA to repetition, going back and checking, looking for meaning in context, and so on all relate to eye movement. Some current instructional models might suggest that children read one phoneme or word at a time, but eye research dating from the 1800s refutes that notion. Eye movement research by Cattell from the late 1800s showed that readers do not look at every word while reading.

Resource B

Example of a Marked Typescript

David
1/27/09

	grasshoppers
101	The Grizzly Spur-throat Grasshopper makes its
102	home in an *a* unusual place for grasshoppers. It doesn't *does not*
103	live in *grass* grasses; it lives in trees! It is rare to see one of
104	these grasshoppers because there are (not) many of
105	them, and they have ©secretive *secret* habits. The
106	Grizzly Spur-throat Grasshopper is a large hopper
107	and © moves \|slowly.\| It camouflages within its tree
108	habitat and is a medium-gray color with dark spots. Ⓡ
109	It (often) seems to disappear against the bark of a tree.
110	This grasshopper lives in eastern hardwood forests and
111	southeastern pine forests. It can also be found on the
112	Midwest prairies. On your next walk in a *pine* forest or
113	through the prairie, Ⓡ look up, and you *just* just might see
114	the Grizzly Spur-throat Grasshopper!

Resource C

Retelling Guide for Narrative Text

Name ____________________ Date ______________________________

Name of Text ____

<u>Directions:</u> Score each of the following unaided retelling responses on a scale of 0–10 depending on the clarity and depth of the student responses. Teachers may wish to have the answers prepared ahead of time to facilitate scoring. These may be stored in the reader's portfolio or with assessment records for RMA or CRMA.

	Aided	Unaided
_____ Identifies key story characters.	_____	_____
_____ Identifies setting.	_____	_____
_____ Identifies story problem (conflict).	_____	_____
_____ Identifies key story episodes.	_____	_____
_____ Identifies problem resolution.	_____	_____

Comments:

SOURCE: Adapted from Moore & Gilles, 2005, with permission.

Resource D

Retelling Guide for Expository Text

Name ____________________ Date ______________________________

Name of Text ____

Directions: Score each of the following unaided retelling responses on a scale of 0–10, depending on the clarity and depth of the student responses. Teachers may wish to have the answers prepared ahead of time to facilitate scoring. These may be stored in the reader's portfolio or with assessment records for RMA or CRMA.

	Aided	Unaided
_____ All important facts are recalled.	_____	_____
_____ Supporting ideas are recalled.	_____	_____
_____ Ideas recalled in logical order.	_____	_____
_____ Reader recalled important conclusions.	_____	_____
_____ Reader stated valid inferences.	_____	_____

Comments:

SOURCE: Adapted from Moore & Gilles, 2005, with permission.

Resource E

Practice Text for Miscue Marking

The Grizzly Spur-throat Grasshopper makes its home in an unusual place for grasshoppers. It doesn't live in grasses; it lives in trees! It is rare to see one of these grasshoppers because there are not many of them, and they have secretive habits. The Grizzly Spur-throat Grasshopper is a large hopper and moves slowly. It camouflages within its tree habitat and is a medium-gray color with dark spots. It often seems to disappear against the bark of a tree. This grasshopper lives in eastern hardwood forests and southeastern pine forests. It can also be found on the Midwest prairies. On your next walk in a forest or through the prairie, look up, and you just might see the Grizzly Spur-throat Grasshopper!

Resource F

Focusing on Miscues: For Student Reference

Omissions: When a word is left out, it will be circled.

Insertions: When a word is added, use a carat to mark it. ∧

Repetitions: When a word is repeated, use a circled *R* to mark it. Ⓡ

Reversals: When words are reversed, use lines to mark it. to remember

Substitutions: When a word is substituted for another, it is written above the text.

Self-corrections: When a word(s) is corrected after a miscue, use a circled *C* to mark it. Ⓒ

Dialect: When dialect or a certain way of speaking affects the pronunciation, mark a ***D*** above the word.

Resource G

Reproducible Simplified Miscue Organizer

RMA Session Organizer I: Simplified Version

Reader ______________________________

Date ______________________________

Name of Text ______________________________

<u>Directions:</u> Write the number of the line of text, the exact text, and the miscue as read. Put a *C* beside the miscue as read if it was self-corrected. Circle a yes or no if the miscue changed the meaning of the sentence.

Line of text	Text	Miscue as Read/*C*	Did the miscue change the meaning?	
________	________	________	Yes	No
________	________	________	Yes	No
________	________	________	Yes	No
________	________	________	Yes	No
________	________	________	Yes	No
________	________	________	Yes	No

<u>Questions to think about:</u>

- Does the miscue make sense?
- Does the miscue change the meaning of the sentence?
- Why do you think the reader miscued?
- What connections to other text or life experiences does the reader make in the retelling?

<u>Some topics for discussion:</u>

SOURCE: Reprinted from *Reading Conversations: Retrospective Miscue Analysis with Struggling Readers Grades 4–12* by Rita Moore and Carol Gilles. Portsmouth, NH: Heinemann Publishers. Copyright 2005.

Resource H

Burke Reading Interview

1. When you are reading and you come to something you don't know, what do you do?

   Do you ever do anything else?

2. Who is a good reader you know?
3. What makes a good reader?
4. Do you think that he or she ever comes to something he or she doesn't know when he or she is reading?
5. If the answer is *yes*: When he or she does come to something he or she doesn't know, what do you think he or she does about it?

   If the answer is *no*: Suppose ________ comes to something he or she doesn't know.

   What do you think he or she would do?

6. If you knew that someone was having difficulty reading, how would you help that person?
7. What would anyone else or your teacher do to help that person?
8. How did you learn to read? What did your teacher or someone else do to help you learn?
9. What would you like to do better as a reader?
10. Do you think you are a good reader? Why or why not?

Moore and Gilles have modified the Burke to add questions 11 and 12.

11. What makes a good reader?
12. What does reading mean to you?

SOURCE: Reprinted from *Reading Miscue Inventory: Alternative Procedures* by Yetta M. Goodman, Dorothy J. Watson, and Carolyn L. Burke. Katonah, NY: Richard C. Owen Publishers, Inc. Copyright 1987. Reprinted by permission. All rights reserved.

Resource I

Thinking About Reading: Reproducible Survey

Name ____ Date ___________

What is reading?

____

____

____

____

____

____

How do you read?

____

____

____

____

____

____

What do you do to read?

____

____

____

____

____

____

____

Resource J

Socratic Circles Reproducible Tracking Sheet

Directions: Outer Circle: Write down a miscue you would like to focus on when it is the Outer Circle's turn to discuss.

Here is the miscue I want to talk about: ______________________________

Record information about the miscue as the Inner Circle discusses.

- Did the miscue change the meaning of the text?
- What does the miscue tell us about what the reader knows about language?
- What was the reader thinking at the time the miscue was read?
- What kinds of connections was the reader making?
- What prior knowledge does the reader have that might have helped understand the text?
- Was the miscue a "smart" or an "okay" miscue?
- What did you notice about the retelling that gives you more information about how the reader made meaning of the text?

References and Resources

Alan, P., & Watson, D. J. (1977). *Findings of research in miscue analysis: Classroom implications.* Urbana, IL: ERIC and National Council of Teachers of English.

Atwell, N. (1998). *In the middle: New understandings about writing, reading, and learning.* 2nd. ed. Portsmouth, NH: Boynton/Cook.

Bandura, A. (1997). *Self-efficacy: The exercise of control.* New York, NY: W. H. Freeman and Company.

Barnes, D. (1975/1992). *From communication to curriculum.* London: Penguin Books.

Barnes, D. R., Britton, J., & Rosen, H. (1969). *Language, the learner, and the school.* London: Penguin.

Barnes, D. R., Britton, N. J., Britton, J., & Torbe, M. (1990). *Language, the learner, and the school,* 4th ed. Portsmouth, NH: Boynton/Cook.

Bloome, D., & Dail, A. R. K. (1997). Toward (re)defining miscue analysis: Reading as a social and cultural process. *Language Arts, 74*(8): 610–617.

Blumenfeld, P. C., & Marx, R. W. (1997). Motivation and cognition. In H. J. Walberg & G. D. Haertel (Eds.), *Multiple perspective analysis of classroom discourse.* Norwood, NJ: Ablex.

Brisk, M., & Harrington, M. (2007). *Literacy and bilingualism: A handbook for all teachers.* Mahwah, NJ: Lawrence Erlbaum.

Burke, C. (1987). Reading interview. In Y. M. Goodman, D. J. Watson, & C. L. Burke (Eds.), *Reading miscue inventory: Alternative procedures.* New York: Richard C. Owen.

Cattell, J. (1886). The time it takes to see and name objects. *Mind, 11,* 62–65.

Christian, B., & Bloome, C. (2004). Learning to read is who you are. *Reading and Writing Quarterly, 20*(4), 365–384.

Clay, M. M. (2000). *Running records for classroom teachers.* Portsmouth, NH: Heinemann.

Copeland, M. (2005). *Socratic circles. Fostering critical and creative thinking in middle and high school.* Portland, ME: Stenhouse.

Costa, A. L. (2008). *The school as a home for the mind* (2nd Ed.). Thousand Oaks, CA: Corwin.

Costello, S. (1992). *Collaborative retrospective miscue analysis with middle school students.* Unpublished doctoral dissertation, University of Arizona, Tucson, AZ.

Costello, S. (1996). A teacher researcher uses RMA. In Y. M. Goodman & A. M. Marek (Eds.), *Retrospective miscue analysis: Revaluing readers and reading.* Katonah, NY: Richard C. Owen.

Davenport, M. R. (1993). Reflecting through talk on content area reading. In K. M. Pierce & C. Gilles (Eds.), *Cycles of meaning: Exploring the potential of talk in learning communities.* Portsmouth, NH: Heinemann.

Davenport, M. R. (2002). *Miscues not mistakes: Reading assessment in the classroom.* Portsmouth, NH: Heinemann.

Davenport, M. R., & Lauritzen, C. (2002). Inviting reflection on reading through over the shoulder miscue analysis. *Language Arts, 80*(2), 109–118.

Davenport, M. R., Lauritzen, C., & Smith, K. (2002). Inviting reflection on reading through over the shoulder miscue analysis. *Language Arts, 80*(2), 109–118.

Delabarre E. B. (1898). A method of recording eye-movements. *Psychological Review, 8*, 572–74.

Duckett, P. (2003). Envisioning story: The eye movements of beginning readers. *Literacy Teaching and Learning, 7*(1), 77–89.

Duckworth, E. (2006). *The having of wonderful ideas.* New York, NY: Teachers College Press.

Dweck, C., & Bempechet, J. (1983). Children's theories of intelligence: Consequences for learning. In S. Paris, B. Olson, & H. Stevenson (Eds.), *Learning and motivation in the classroom.* Hillsdale, NJ: Lawrence Erlbaum.

Fletcher, R., & Portalupi, J. (2001). *Writing workshop: The essential guide.* Portsmouth, NH: Heinemann.

Folger, T. (2001). *Readers' parallel text construction while talking and thinking about the reading process.* Unpublished doctoral dissertation, University of Missouri-Columbia.

Fountas, I., & Pinnell, G. S. (1996). *Guided reading: Good first teaching for all children.* Portsmouth, NH: Heinemann.

Freeman, D., & Freeman, Y. (2006). *Teaching reading and writing in Spanish and English in bilingual and dual language classrooms.* Portsmouth, NH: Heinemann.

Gilles, C., & Dickinson, J. (2000). Rejoining the literacy club: Valuing middle grade readers. *Language Arts, 77*(6), 512–522.

Goodman, D. (1996). The Reading Detective Club. In Y. M. Goodman & A. M. Marek (Eds.) *Retrospective miscue analysis: Revaluing readers and reading.* Katonah, NY: Richard C. Owen.

Goodman, K. S. (1968). *Study of children's behavior while reading orally* (Contract No. OE-610–136). Washington, D. C.: Department of Health, Education, and Welfare.

Goodman, K. S. (1969). Linguistics in a relevant curriculum. *Education, 89*, 303–306.

Goodman, K. S. (1973). Miscues: Windows on the reading process. In K. S. Goodman (Ed.) *Miscue analysis: Applications to reading instruction.* Urbana, IL: ERIC Clearinghouse on Reading and Communication Skills and the National Council of Teachers of English.

Goodman, K. S. (1984). Unity in reading. In A. C. Purves & O. Niles (Eds.) *Becoming readers in a complex society.* Chicago: University of Chicago Press.

Goodman, K. S. (1994). Reading, writing, and written texts: A transactional socio psycholinguistic view. In R. B. Ruddell, M. R. Ruddell, & H. Singer (Eds.)

Theoretical models and process of reading (4th ed.). Newark, DE: National Council of Teachers of English.

Goodman, K. S. (1996a). *Ken Goodman: On reading.* Portsmouth, NH: Heinemann.

Goodman, K. S. (1996b). Principles of revaluing. In Y. M. Goodman & A. M. Marek (Eds.), *Retrospective miscue analysis: Revaluing readers and reading.* Katonah, NY: Richard C. Owen.

Goodman, Y. M. (1995). Miscue analysis for classroom teachers: Some history and some procedures. *Primary Voices K–6, 3*(4), 2–9.

Goodman, Y. M. (1996). Revaluing readers while readers revalue themselves: Retrospective miscue analysis. *The Reading Teacher, 49*(8), 600–609.

Goodman, Y. M. (2003). *Valuing language study: Inquiry into language for elementary and middle schools.* NCTE: Urbana, IL.

Goodman, Y. M. (2007). Online discussion with Yetta Goodman. *Miscue analysis and reading strategies: Past, present, and future.* Katonah, NY: Richard C. Owen.

Goodman, Y. M., & Flurkey, A. (1996). Retrospective miscue analysis in the middle school. In Y. M. Goodman & A. M. Marek (Eds.) *Retrospective miscue analysis: Revaluing readers and reading.* Katonah, NY: Richard C. Owen.

Goodman, Y. M., & Marek, A. M. (1989). *Retrospective miscue analysis: Two papers* (Occasional Paper No. 19). Tucson, AZ: University of Arizona, College of Education, Program in Language and Literacy.

Goodman, Y. M., & Marek, A M. (1996). *Retrospective miscue analysis: Revaluing readers and reading.* Katonah, NY: Richard C. Owen.

Goodman, Y. M., Watson, D. J., & Burke, C. L. (1987). *Reading miscue inventory: Alternative procedures.* New York: Richard C. Owen.

Goodman, Y. M., Watson, D. J., & Burke, C. L. (2005). *Reading miscue inventory: From evaluation to instruction for all readers.* New York: Richard C. Owen.

Gore, J. (1992). What we can do for you! What *can* 'we' do for 'you'?: Struggling over empowerment in critical and feminist pedagogy. In C. Luke & J. Gore (Eds.) *Feminisms and critical pedagogy.* New York: Routledge.

Gore, J. (1993). *The struggle for pedagogies.* New York: Routledge.

Halliday, M. A. K. (1980). Three aspects of children's language development: Learning language, learning through language, learning about language. In Y. Goodman, M. Haussler, & D. Strickland (Eds.) *Oral and Written Language Development Research: Impact on the Schools.* Urbana, IL: IRA and NCTE joint publications.

Harp, B. (2000). *The handbook of literacy assessment and evaluation* (2nd ed.). Norwood, MA: Christopher-Gordon.

Harp, B. (2006). The handbook of literacy assessment and evaluation (3rd ed.). Norwood, MA: Christopher-Gordon.

Hudelson, S. (1984). Kan yu ret an rayt en ingles: Children become literate in English as a second language. *TESOL Quarterly, 18*, 221–237.

International Reading Association. (2008, June/July). IRA issues statement on Reading First report. *Reading Today, 25*(6). pp. 1, 4.

Johnston, P. (1997). *Knowing literacy.* Portland, ME: Stenhouse.

Johnston, P. (2004). *Choice words: How our language affects children's learning.* York, ME: Stenhouse.

Keene, E., & Zimmermann, S. (1997). *Mosaic of thought.* Portsmouth, NH: Heinemann.

Keene, E., & Zimmermann, S. (2007). *Mosaic of thought* (2nd ed.). Portsmouth, NH: Heinemann.

Lauritzen, C. (Spring, 2009). A new literacy panel report: What does it tell us? *The Oracle, 25*(3), 11.

Leslie, L., & Caldwell, J. (1988). *Qualitative reading inventory.* New York: Harper Collins.

Lindfors, J. (1991). *Children's language and learning.* Needham Heights, MA: Allyn and Bacon.

Marek, A. M. (1987). *Retrospective miscue analysis as an instructional strategy with adult readers.* Unpublished doctoral dissertation, University of Arizona, Tucson, AZ.

Martens, P. (1998). Using retrospective miscue analysis to inquire: Learning from Michael. *Reading Teacher, 52*(2), 176–80.

McDonald, K. (2008). *What are the effects of using retrospective miscue analysis with students with physical or otherwise health impairments?* Retrieved August 15, 2008, from ProQuest Digital Dissertations. (AAT 3315600).

Moline, S. (1995). *I see what you mean.* Portland, ME: Stenhouse.

Moore, R. A., & Aspegren, C. (2000). *Reaching troubled readers with RMA.* Paper presented at the annual meeting of the International Reading Association, Indianapolis, IN.

Moore, R. A., & Aspegren, C. (2001). Reflective conversations between two learners: Retrospective miscue analysis. *Journal of Adolescent and Adult Literacy, 44*(6), 492–503.

Moore, R. A., & Brantingham, K. (2003). Nathan: A case study in retrospective miscue analysis. *Reading Teacher, 56*(5), 466–474.

Moore, R. A., & Gilles, C. (2005). *Reading conversations.* Portsmouth, NH: Heinemann.

Paulson, E. & Freeman, A. (2003). *Insight from the eyes: The science of effective reading instruction.* Portsmouth, NH: Heinemann.

Pahls-Weiss, M. (2004). A study of the use of retrospective miscue analysis with selected first grade readers. Unpublished doctoral dissertation, University of Missouri-Columbia, 2004.

Pearson, P. D., & Gallagher, M. C. (1983). The instruction of reading comprehension. *Contemporary Educational Psychology, 8*, 317–344.

Pierce, K., & Gilles, C. (Eds.). (1993). *Cycles of meaning: Exploring the potential of talk in learning communities.* Portsmouth, NH: Heinemann.

Pinnell, G. S., & Fountes, I. (2000). *Word matters.* Portsmouth, NH: Heinemann.

Rosenblatt, L. (1938/1976). *Literature as exploration.* New York: Noble and Noble.

Rosenblatt, L. (1978). *The reader, the text, the poem: The transactional theory of the literary work.* Carbondale, IL: Southern Illinois University Press.

Sibberson, F., & Szymusiak, K. (2003). *Still learning to read: Teaching students in grades 3–6.* Portland, ME: Stenhouse.

Smith, F. (1994). *Understanding reading: A psycholinguistic analysis of reading and learning to read* (5th ed.). Hillsdale, NJ: Erlbaum.

Strickland, K., & Strickland, J. (2000). *Making assessment elementary.* Portsmouth, NH: Heinemann.

Taberski, S. (2000). *On solid ground: Strategies for teaching reading K–3* [DVD]. Portsmouth, NH: Heinemann.

Taberski, S. (2008). *A close-up look at teaching reading: Focusing on children and our goals* [DVD]. Portsmouth, NH: Heinemann.

Tovani, C. (2000). *I read it, but I don't get it.* New York, NY: Stenhouse.

U.S. Department of Education. (2008). *Reading first impact study: Interim report executive summary* (NCEE 2008–4019).

Vacca, R., & Vacca, J. A. (2007). *Content area reading.* New York, NY: Allyn and Bacon.

Vygotsky, L. (1978). *Mind in society: The development of higher psychological processes.* Cambridge, MA: Harvard University Press.

Watson, D. (2008, July). Where do we go from here: From miscues to strategies. Paper presented at the annual meeting of the Whole Language Umbrella (NCTE), Tucson, AZ.

Watson, D. J. (1978). Reader-selected miscues: Getting more from sustained silent reading. *English Education, 10,* 75–85.

Watson, D. J. (1988). Knowing where we're coming from. In C. Gilles, M. Bixby, P. Crowley, M. Henrichs, F. Reynolds, & D. Pyle (Eds.), *Whole language strategies for secondary students.* New York: Richard C. Owen.

Watson, D. J. (1996a). Miscue analysis for teachers. In S. Wilde (Ed.), *Making a difference: Selected writings of Dorothy Watson.* Portsmouth, NH: Heinemann.

Watson, D. J. (1996b). Miscues we have known and loved. In S. Wilde (Ed.), *Making a difference: Selected writings of Dorothy Watson.* Portsmouth, NH: Heinemann.

Watson, D. J. (1996c). Watching and listening to children read. In S. Wilde (Ed.), *Making a difference: Selected writings of Dorothy Watson. Portsmouth,* NH: Heinemann.

Watson, D. J., & Hoge, S. (1996). Reader Selected Miscues. In Y. M. Goodman & A. M. Marek (Eds.), *Retrospective miscue analysis: Revaluing readers and reading.* Katonah, NY: Richard C. Owen.

Weaver, C. (1980). *Psycholinguistics and reading: From process to practice.* Cambridge, Mass.: Winthrop Publisher.

Weaver, C. (1994). *Reading process and practice: From socio-psycholinguistics to whole language.* Portsmouth, NH: Heinemann.

Weaver, C., Gillmeister-Krause, L., & Vento-Zogby, G. (1996). *Creating support for effective literacy instruction.* Portsmouth, NH: Heinemann.

Wells, G. (1986). *The meaning makers: Children learning language and using language to learn.* Portsmouth, NH: Heinemann.

Wells, G., & Chang-Wells, L. (1992). *Constructing knowledge together: Classrooms as centers of inquiry and literacy.* Portsmouth, NH: Heinemann.

Whitmore, K., & Crowell, C. (1994). *Inventing a classroom: Life in a bilingual, whole language learning community.* Portland, ME: Stenhouse.

Wilde, S. (2000). *Miscue analysis made easy: Building on student strengths.* Portsmouth, NH: Heinemann.

Wilson, J. (2005). Interrupting the failure cycle: Revaluing two seventh-grade struggling readers. *Voices From the Middle, 12*(4), 25–30.

Wollman-Bonilla, J. (2000). *Family message journals: Teaching writing through family involvement.* Urbana, IL: National Council of Teachers of English.

Worsnop, C. (1980). *A procedure for using the technique of the reading miscue inventories as a remedial teaching tool with adolescents* (ERIC Document ED 324644).

Worsnop, C. (1996). The beginnings of retrospective miscue analysis. In Y. M. Goodman & A. M. Marek (Eds.). *Retrospective miscue analysis: Revaluing readers and reading.* Katonah, NH: Richard C. Owen.

References for Children's Literature

Bridges, R. (1999). *Through my eyes: Ruby Bridges.* Lundell, M. (Ed.). New York, NY: Scholastic.

Davidson, M. (1971). *Louis Braille: The boy who invented books for the blind.* New York, NY: Scholastic.

George, J. C. (2001). *My side of the mountain.* Penguin Young Readers Group. London, English: Puffin Books.

Graff, S., & Graff, P. A. (1965). *Helen Keller: Crusader for the blind and deaf.* New York, NY: Bantam Doubleday Dell Books for Young Readers.

Hopkins, T. (2004). A tree-dwelling grasshopper discovered on the Konza Prairie! Tallgrass Gazette. Retrieved from: http//keep.konza.ksu.edu/docents/tgg/tgg_spg04.pdf

Madden, M. W. (2003). Lewis and Clark in Kansas. *Kansas Kaleidoscope,* Special Issue, Kansas State Historical Society.

Markle, S. (1994). *Outside and inside spiders.* New York, NY: Bradbury Press.

Mathis, S. B. (1986). *The hundred penny box.* New York: Puffin Newbery Library Series.

Myers, L. (2002). *Lewis and Clark and me: A dog's tale.* Baltimore, MD: Henry Holt & Company.

Selznick, B. (2007). *The invention of Hugo Cabret.* New York: Scholastic.

Spinelli, J. (1990). *Maniac Magee.* Boston, MA: Little, Brown, & Company.

Warner, G. C. (1989). *The boxcar children.* Morton Grove, IL: Albert Whitman Company.

Wilson, C. (2001). *Rosa Parks biography.* New York: Scholastic Paperbacks.

Index

CORWIN
A SAGE Company

The Corwin logo—a raven striding across an open book—represents the union of courage and learning. Corwin is committed to improving education for all learners by publishing books and other professional development resources for those serving the field of PreK–12 education. By providing practical, hands-on materials, Corwin continues to carry out the promise of its motto: **"Helping Educators Do Their Work Better."**